KITCHEN
UPGRADES

EDITORS OF
FineHomebuilding

The Taunton Press

The Taunton Press
Inspiration for hands-on living®

The Taunton Press, Inc., 63 South Main Street, PO Box 5506, Newtown, CT 06470-5506
e-mail: tp@taunton.com

Editor: Christina Glennon
Copy editor: Seth Reichgott
Indexer: Jim Curtis
Cover design: Guido Caroti
Interior design: Carol Singer
Layout: Susan Lampe-Wilson
Cover photographers: Front cover (clockwise from top left): Susan Teare, Debra Judge Silber, John Gruen,
    Back cover (left to right): Patrick McCombe, Justin Fink

LIBRARY OF CONGRESS CATALOGING-IN-PUBLICATION DATA

Names: Taunton Press, author.
Title: Kitchen upgrades / editors of Fine homebuilding.
Other titles: Fine Homebuilding.
Description: Newtown, CT : The Taunton Press, Inc., [2017] | Includes index.
Identifiers: LCCN 2016045166 | ISBN 9781631868450
Subjects: LCSH: Kitchens--Remodeling--Amateurs' manuals.
Classification: LCC TH4816.3.K58 K5824 2017 | DDC 643/.30288--dc23
LC record available at https://lccn.loc.gov/2016045166

PRINTED IN THE UNITED STATES OF AMERICA
10 9 8 7 6 5 4 3 2 1

ACKNOWLEDGMENTS

Special thanks to the authors, editors, art directors, copy editors, and other staff members of *Fine Homebuilding* who contributed to the development of the articles in this book.

Contents

A kitchen remodel is among the most exciting improvement projects a homeowner is likely to experience. Such work touches the very core of our homes and how we live in them, and so the upgrades we make in these spaces are impactful in ways that changes to more-private or peripheral rooms are not. After all, the kitchen is where we socialize with our friends and family, where food is prepared and shared with loved ones, and where family plans are formed and dreams are discussed. These are lofty demands placed on spaces that also have to be incredibly functional and as resilient and durable as possible. When done well, a kitchen remodel can bring a uniquely rewarding level of comfort and joy into your home. As easily as a well-designed and well-built kitchen can enhance the experience of home, though, a poorly designed or poorly built kitchen can cause tremendous frustration. It's with this understanding that this book was put together.

The following pages are packed with inspiring design ideas to help guide you toward your dream kitchen. However, inspiration only goes so far with work of this scale and complexity. This edition of *Kitchen Upgrades* is aimed to inspire, but even more so, it's created to inform and empower. We've included practical design lessons to help ensure that you generate the best possible layout for your kitchen and the way your family uses the space. We've curated the best how-to content from *Fine Homebuilding* to help you accomplish tasks such as building a custom island, tiling a backsplash, installing crown molding, and more. This information will help you preserve your budget by allowing you to do the work yourself, and it will help ensure that the work gets done right so you don't have to worry about the quality of the craftsmanship years down the road.

An extensive kitchen remodel is exciting, but we recognize that it can be a bit daunting, too. That is why the information in this book has been sourced from some of North America's best and most talented designers and builders. Trust the information in this book, and know that you're in good hands.

Rob Yagid, Editor, *Fine Homebuilding*

PART 1

Planning and Design

Opening Up
a Kitchen

BY REID HIGHLEY AND JIM COMPTON

Hurried lifestyles have made it necessary for the functions of the kitchen and the main living areas of a house to overlap. In addition to cooking, kitchens have become places for dining, entertaining, working, paying bills, and studying. The ascendancy of the kitchen is a relatively recent development, however, and homes only a few decades old are likely to have cramped kitchens with little connection to the rest of the house.

Fortunately, many of these dated kitchens can be improved with relative ease. The kitchen pictured below is typical of what you might find in an original

ORIGINAL PLAN

Dining room

Living room

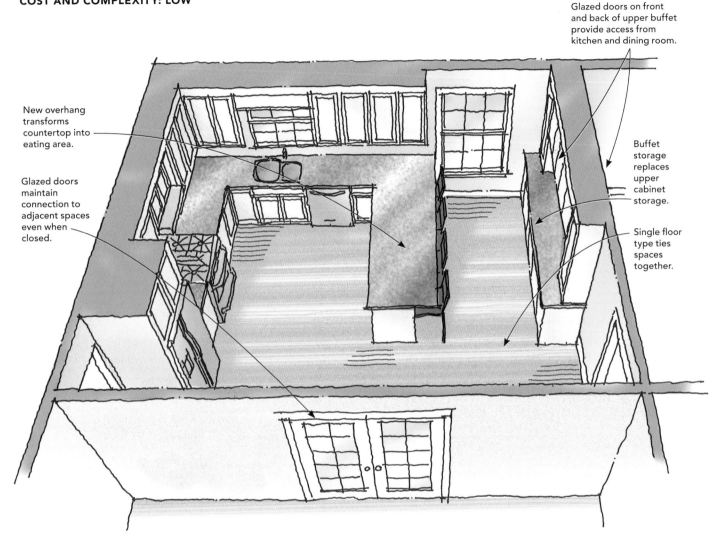

Glazed doors on front and back of upper buffet provide access from kitchen and dining room.

New overhang transforms countertop into eating area.

Glazed doors maintain connection to adjacent spaces even when closed.

Buffet storage replaces upper cabinet storage.

Single floor type ties spaces together.

suburban home built in the 1970s. The sketches that follow illustrate three strategies for reconfiguring this kitchen to make it an open, multifunctional space. While your project won't have this exact layout, the three approaches illustrated here are easily modified, and they offer valuable insight into the potential that lies within remodels of various costs and levels of complexity.

Cost and Complexity: Low

The existing kitchen is kept intact, but a more open feel is achieved by removing the ceiling-hung cabinetry. This makes the room feel larger and facilitates interaction between the cook and those in the eating area. The storage capacity lost by eliminating the cabinets is offset with a built-in buffet that has a pass-through window to the dining room. The top of the buffet has glass doors on both sides to share light with the dining room. To unify the kitchen, new hardwood flooring is installed throughout the room. The existing cased opening is replaced by a 5-ft.-wide pair of glazed French doors to create a better connection to the living room.

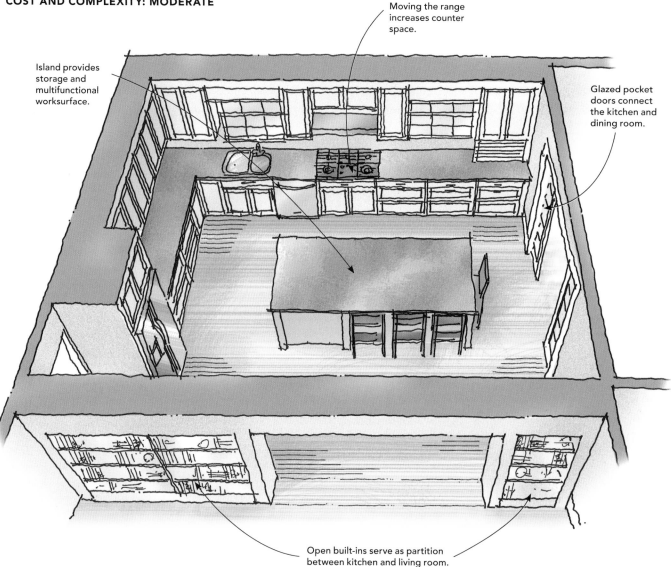

Moving the range increases counter space.

Island provides storage and multifunctional worksurface.

Glazed pocket doors connect the kitchen and dining room.

Open built-ins serve as partition between kitchen and living room.

Cost and Complexity: Moderate

The breakfast area is annexed into the kitchen by removing the peninsula and ceiling cabinets. The cabinetry at the sink wall is extended, significantly increasing storage capacity. The range is moved to the middle of that wall, creating a long run of valuable counter space, and a large island provides eat-in functionality. To enhance the connection to the living room, a large opening that matches the width of the island is created. This opening is treated as a transition zone between the rooms and is enhanced with open shelving, which is handy for stashing cookbooks or displaying fine china. Though the flooring surface is hardwood in both the kitchen and the living room, a wide, flush wood threshold between the rooms provides a delineation of spaces. A wide opening with pocket doors is centered on the short side of the island to make an elegant connection to the formal dining room.

Cost and Complexity: High

A flush header installed in the ceiling creates a continuous plane between the kitchen and the living room and allows removal of the wall that separates the spaces. This plan demands visual organization, so the cabinetry is laid out in an elongated U that wraps three sides of the room. The cabinetry cradles a large island with a sink at its center. The island acts as a visual marker of the transition from the living area to the kitchen. Large pendants suspended over the island will help to reinforce this transition. A cooktop with a decorative tile backsplash is aligned with the sink and becomes the kitchen's focal point. Tall cabinets for the wall ovens and the refrigerator bookend the cabinetry and countertops. New hardwood flooring helps tie the kitchen and the living room together.

COST AND COMPLEXITY: HIGH

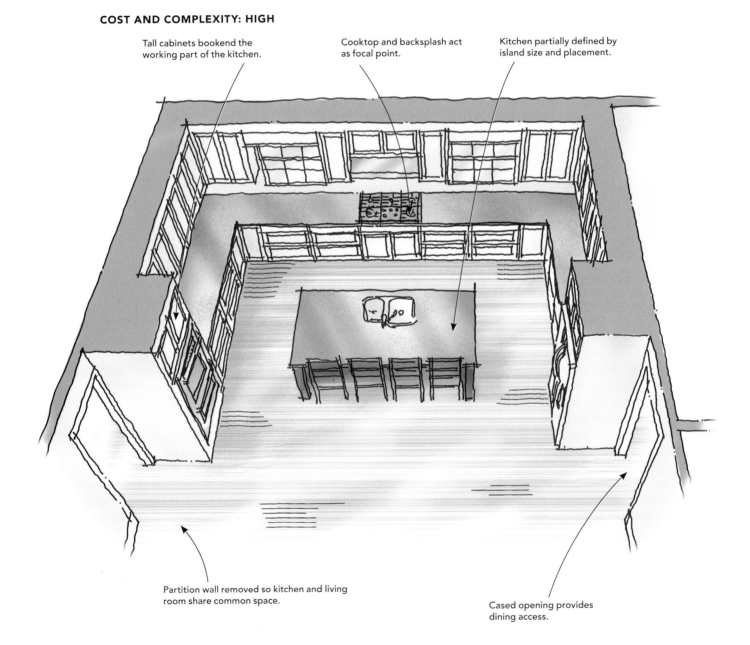

Tall cabinets bookend the working part of the kitchen.

Cooktop and backsplash act as focal point.

Kitchen partially defined by island size and placement.

Partition wall removed so kitchen and living room share common space.

Cased opening provides dining access.

Zones for Small Appliances

BY BUD DIETRICH

Cooking zone

Best thought of as a small-appliance corral, this zone can be outfitted with custom cabinetry for convenient access and storage of your most regularly used items.

Prep zone

A 4-ft. by 10-ft. island is the ideal platform for the prep zone. Centrally located, this is going to be the kitchen's workhorse in terms of meal prep and entertaining.

Breakfast zone

This is the equivalent of the kitchen's drive-through window. Fast meals and beverages are made in this space, which is intended to serve families on the go.

At some point, most of us have been told that to design a kitchen well, we must get the work triangle correct. For me, however, the triangle concept—which is driven largely by the arrangement of the kitchen's major appliances—is a bit antiquated. Sure, it was appropriate for the days when kitchens had to satisfy only three jobs—storage, cooking, and cleanup—but those simple days and those simple kitchens are behind us.

In addition to the major appliances, many modern kitchens are stocked with a handful of small appliances that serve a variety of very specific purposes. Instead of shoehorning these items into kitchen cabinets as an afterthought or simply loading the countertops with them, I anticipate them by proposing kitchen designs that have established zones for small-appliance storage and room for their associated tasks. Here are three such zones to consider for your kitchen design.

THE COOKING ZONE

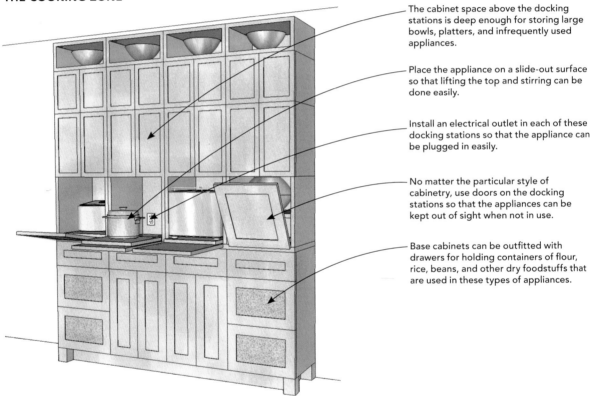

The cabinet space above the docking stations is deep enough for storing large bowls, platters, and infrequently used appliances.

Place the appliance on a slide-out surface so that lifting the top and stirring can be done easily.

Install an electrical outlet in each of these docking stations so that the appliance can be plugged in easily.

No matter the particular style of cabinetry, use doors on the docking stations so that the appliances can be kept out of sight when not in use.

Base cabinets can be outfitted with drawers for holding containers of flour, rice, beans, and other dry foodstuffs that are used in these types of appliances.

The Cooking Zone

From the rice cooker to the waffle maker to the slow cooker, you should be able to access all of your small cooking appliances easily, use them as needed, clean them up, and store them with the least amount of effort possible. Because this category of appliances can be sizable in many homes, it's important to consider the appliances that are used most frequently and to design this zone to accommodate them. For example, if you use the slow cooker a lot,

you'll want to make sure that this appliance is in a place where it can be slid out of its cabinet, turned on, and left to cook.

Small cooking appliances that have only occasional use also need to be stored. The cabinet for them does not need to be deep; 16 in. to 18 in. should be plenty. It doesn't have to be too large, either. A unit of about 6 lin. ft. should accommodate docking stations for three or four appliances.

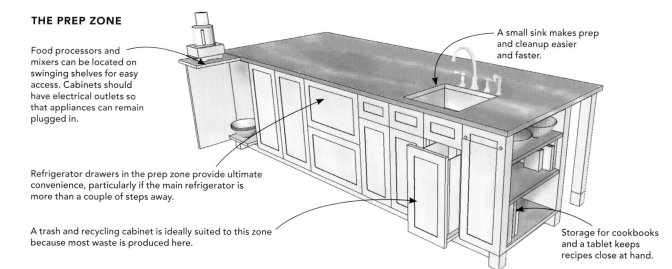

THE PREP ZONE

Food processors and mixers can be located on swinging shelves for easy access. Cabinets should have electrical outlets so that appliances can remain plugged in.

A small sink makes prep and cleanup easier and faster.

Refrigerator drawers in the prep zone provide ultimate convenience, particularly if the main refrigerator is more than a couple of steps away.

A trash and recycling cabinet is ideally suited to this zone because most waste is produced here.

Storage for cookbooks and a tablet keeps recipes close at hand.

The Prep Zone

From the food processor to the mixer, many of us slice, dice, mix, and blend routinely. You can stow all of these appliances in deep base cabinets and lug them out when you need them, or you can allow them and their snaking cords to clutter your countertops; you don't have to, though. Instead, integrate a prep zone close to the refrigerator and the cooking area.

Locating this zone at an island and between the refrigerator and prime cooking area is ideal. The chef then will be able to pivot between tasks and have everything within arm's reach. This means placing these small appliances in the base cabinets that make up the island. The island should be a good size if you wish to accommodate entertaining and food prep at the same time.

The Breakfast Zone

The days of the big breakfast are long gone. With everyone's hectic work and school schedules, it's a wonder we have time to make a morning meal at all. Dedicating an area to preparing grab-and-go cups of coffee, bowls of cereal, or toast can make a kitchen work more efficiently. A zone like this needs roughly 6 ft. of base cabinets and countertops, with corresponding upper cabinets. This run of cabinets will accommodate a 24-in.-wide undercounter refrigerator as well as a small sink. There should be

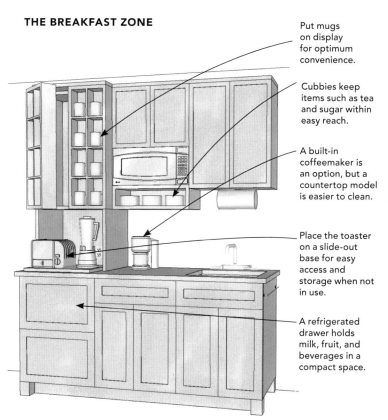

THE BREAKFAST ZONE

Put mugs on display for optimum convenience.

Cubbies keep items such as tea and sugar within easy reach.

A built-in coffeemaker is an option, but a countertop model is easier to clean.

Place the toaster on a slide-out base for easy access and storage when not in use.

A refrigerated drawer holds milk, fruit, and beverages in a compact space.

a deep upper cabinet—say 16 in.—at one end of this area for housing the toaster and a blender or juicer.

This area can be tailored to serve as a beverage zone as well, enabling you to make smoothies in the morning and margaritas in the evening without disrupting the chef in the center of the kitchen.

Choosing Countertops

BY JAMIE GOLD

There is no one-size-fits-all countertop for every kitchen, just as there is no one-size-fits-all kitchen for every home. When I began working as a designer close to a decade ago, most clients came to me wanting granite countertops. They ogled the large island covered in granite that we had on display—where no one ever cooked, chopped vegetables, mixed drinks, did homework, worked on art projects, or cleaned up after dinner.

Looking rich and beautiful is easy if you never do a day's work. It's harder for countertops subjected to the rigors of a family's daily living, especially spills, splatters, and flying projectiles. I design kitchens with an approach I call "sensible style." Its first principle is that your kitchen needs to fit how you really live.

The second sensible-style principle is that your new kitchen should honor the home it's being installed in; this means that your new countertops should complement the overall style and materials of the areas that surround the kitchen, as well as those in the kitchen itself. I've seen too many homeowners—and even some industry pros—choose a countertop without considering its maintenance requirements, durability, material properties such as softness or porosity, warranty, or even the way a pattern might play against neighboring surfaces such as kitchen cabinetry and flooring. My goal here is to help you avoid making such design mistakes.

Establish a Design Process

Kitchen countertops should never be chosen on the basis of looks alone. First, consider the needs and the lifestyle of your family. Take into account habits and any physical limitations. Once you've done that, then you'll be ready to choose the type of material that will top your cabinets for the next 10 or 20 years.

The first elements to consider when choosing the look you want for your tops are the other major surfaces in the kitchen. I often start with the floor, which may extend beyond the kitchen and, in a remodel, may already be in place. Cabinets and appliances are also major aesthetic considerations. What is their color, style, and pattern? Is there just one cabinet finish to coordinate with, or several? (I keep a consistent top if the cabinet finishes vary.) How will the appliances look next to the tops? Is there too much contrast, or not enough?

(continued on p. 18)

SUITS ITS SPACE. In this midcentury San Diego kitchen I designed with the architect-homeowner and a colleague, we used family-friendly engineered stone—also known as quartz—for the countertops. Its soft color and pebbly pattern coordinate handsomely with the floors' driftwood-gray finish, the glossy-white cabinets, and the oceanic touches throughout the surrounding spaces. The material evokes the nearby tide pools, where the family enjoys walking and which are visible from the adjacent living room.

EIGHT GREAT COUNTERTOPS

ENGINEERED STONE/QUARTZ

This is my go-to kitchen countertop, specified for more of my projects than any other material. It's durable; low maintenance; and heat-, stain-, and scratch-resistant. I tend toward solid neutral colors, and I love the new soft-matte finishes such as Silestone®'s Suede (pictured).

WOOD

Warm and elegant, a wood top by a company such as Craft-Art® (pictured) can add unsurpassed beauty to a kitchen. I adore the look of wood countertops—particularly walnut on painted cabinets in a traditional kitchen. I'm less enamored with wood in food-prep or cooking zones.

DEKTON

This is the newest entrant in the countertop marketplace. Dekton® is a composite of three of my top countertop materials—quartz, glass, and porcelain—and it embodies their durability, heat resistance, scratch resistance, and low maintenance.

SOLID-SURFACE ACRYLIC AND ACRYLIC BLENDS

Tops such as Avonite® (pictured) have a soft, low-glare, easy-care surface ideal for aging-in-place kitchens. I also like the material's seamless appearance. This material does have a few downsides: It can be scratched or scorched easily, and it rarely succeeds at looking as good as natural materials. Also, its cost is comparable to that of granite or quartz.

SLAB GLASS

Glass is extremely durable; it's heat- and damage-resistant with normal use. It's also a surface that can add exceptional drama to a kitchen, especially when it's underlit. Its major downside is cost, which puts it out of reach for projects that would use it for anything other than a small accent.

CONCRETE

Concrete is versatile and comes in virtually any color combination and pattern. Slab concrete, made by manufacturers such as the Concrete Collaborative® (pictured) is nearly flawless in appearance. I like its industrial look for contemporary kitchens, but not its need for regular sealing.

PORCELAIN AND CERAMIC SLABS

Recently, I came across an Italian line, Iris (pictured), that looks like marble, but without its softness or porosity. There is also the Iron Series from Spain's The Size. Like any porcelain or ceramic surface, these countertops are durable and low maintenance. You can have an integral sink in the same pattern if you'd like, but the only edge profile offered is a bevel.

RECYCLED GLASS

Recycled-glass countertops by companies such as Vetrazzo® (pictured) are made from bottles, windows, and other castoffs blended with cement to create smooth slabs with fun back-stories. Because most of it needs to be sealed, I like this dramatic material as a focal-point countertop away from food-prep or cooking zones.

MATCHING SURFACES. The wood counter on the kitchen's buffet closely resembles the color and tone of the wood flooring throughout the kitchen and adjoining spaces. This countertop helps connect the kitchen to the rest of the house and is a suitable material for a space that will not have to withstand the abuse of a hardworking prep space.

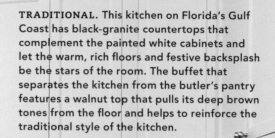

TRADITIONAL. This kitchen on Florida's Gulf Coast has black-granite countertops that complement the painted white cabinets and let the warm, rich floors and festive backsplash be the stars of the room. The buffet that separates the kitchen from the butler's pantry features a walnut top that pulls its deep brown tones from the floor and helps to reinforce the traditional style of the kitchen.

CLASSIC CONTRAST. The black-granite countertops on the working side of the kitchen are offset by white cabinets and bright-blue backsplash tiles. The tops were selected for their durability and subtleness.

Regardless of whether you pick color A or pattern B, you need to choose the type of material before the cabinetry design is completed. Your countertops may require special sink accommodations, or supports may need to be factored into the cabinet design and construction.

In many of the spaces I design from scratch, cabinets are chosen first, then countertops and appliances, then flooring, then wall coverings. Other designers start with flooring and work their way up to the counters. The order is less important than taking a holistic approach.

Matching the Top to the Use

Not all kitchens are used the same way. Some functionality issues I ask clients about include the type of food preparation and cooking they do on a regular basis. I ask how often they entertain, and if they do so formally or casually. I ask where in the kitchen they like to chop vegetables, trim meat, or mix drinks. I also want to know if they help children with homework in the kitchen, or bathe pets or babies, or fold laundry.

It's also important to ask user-oriented questions. For instance, does anyone who uses the kitchen have reduced vision, a balance impairment, or a memory limitation?

Homes with seniors can benefit from an acrylic or acrylic-blend countertop such as Corian® or Avonite. These surfaces feel softer when struck by someone with depth-perception or balance problems, and they are reparable if a shaking hand with a knife misses the cutting board or a memory-challenged user sets a hot pot down on the bare surface. These materials are also nonporous, which reduces the risk of food contamination, and they are maintenance-free.

Because of its durability, low maintenance, and stain resistance, I often specify engineered stone for families with active children. An acrylic material

can fit the bill, too, given its repairability. Porcelain- and ceramic-slab tops are also good family-friendly alternatives for their durability and minimal maintenance demands.

Create a Cohesive Style

Kitchens tend to fall into one of four primary styles: traditional, contemporary or modern, transitional, and eclectic. Transitional kitchens are my favorite, as they blend many of the classic elements of traditional kitchens, such as crown molding and decorative hardware, with the simpler aesthetic of modern kitchens, such as simple hardware and streamlined, nonfussy door styles.

The countertop you choose should fit the overall style of the space. For example, wood can be butcher block for a casual transitional kitchen's food-prep area, or it can be elegant planks for a more formal buffet. Glass can be a slab for a contemporary cooking zone, or it can be a recycled blend for an eclectic focal-point bar. Metal options include zinc or copper for a traditional space, or stainless steel for a contemporary kitchen with next to no upkeep. Stone, such as marble, soapstone, or granite, is common for a traditional home whose owners don't mind the extra care. Quartz can be a good choice for the working surfaces of just about any style of kitchen, given the wide range of solids and patterns available. Finally, there's concrete, which can be poured or installed as a slab.

You also need to choose the right color, finish, and pattern to work with your kitchen's overall style and adjacent materials. I like to pull a dominant color from the floor for the countertop or go with a pattern or solid that will complement it. If everything's a focal point, nothing's a focal point.

Kitchens with high-gloss, solid-colored cabinets—white is popular—pair well with either low-sheen or textured tops. If the floor is glossy concrete or terrazzo, I opt for a top with some texture, such as a linen-look porcelain slab, to make the space feel less slick. If the floor is wood or bamboo, a solid-colored or lightly patterned quartz works well.

You have more choices than ever in today's marketplace, including old favorites such as wood and stone, and newer materials such as engineered stone, porcelain and ceramic slab, and concrete.

If you start your decision-making process from the standpoint of what works for how you live, whom you live with, and what you live in, rather than which online image you loved last week, your countertop choice is more likely to serve you well in the long run.

SOURCES

ENGINEERED STONE/QUARTZ
www.caesarstoneus.com
www.cambriausa.com
www.silestoneusa.com

DEKTON
www.dekton.com/usa

SLAB GLASS
www.thinkglass.com

CONCRETE
www.concrete-collaborative
.com

WOOD
www.craft-art.com
www.glumber.com
(Grothouse)
www.jaaronwoodcountertops
.com

SOLID-SURFACE ACRYLIC AND ACRYLIC BLENDS
www.avonite.com
www.corian.com
www.staron.com

PORCELAIN AND CERAMIC SLABS
www.thesize.es
www.tpbarcelona.com
www.irisceramica.com

RECYCLED GLASS
www.eos-surfaces.com
(GEOS)
www.icestoneusa.com
www.vetrazzo.com

Mixing Countertop Materials

BY DEBRA JUDGE SILBER

Flip, swipe, or click your way through any kitchen photo gallery, and you'll notice quickly that using more than one countertop material has become the norm. The continued popularity of islands, exposure to an array of intriguing new materials online, and the expectation that a good kitchen fills multiple roles—with its countertops serving as the playing field for activities as diverse as cooking, socializing, and bill paying—all push designers and homeowners to think beyond a single surface that does it all.

And why not? Mixing materials not only presents creative opportunities, but it ensures the most sensible surface for a particular area's assigned use. After all, the qualities we require in a surface used for chopping carrots are far different from those we value in the peninsula where we sip coffee or the counter that holds the dish drain. And function is just one issue to consider.

The Subtle Language of Surfaces

Kitchens come in lots of styles—from traditional to contemporary, from farmhouse to midcentury. Because countertops represent so much visual real estate, the material they're made of can exert a strong influence on—even make or break—a

A NATURAL BALANCE. Connecticut designer Rafe Churchill's traditional focus leads him to pair natural materials such as wood and stone that have markedly different qualities. "Very often we will do the perimeter cabinets in stone and the island in a 'food prep' wood surface—a surface ready for direct cutting and typical kitchen work," he says. The wood surface shown here and on the facing page is maple with a food-safe oil finish. The perimeter cabinets are topped with soapstone and include an integrated sink.

SUPPORTING ROLE. In this kitchen, a subdued perimeter of Blanco Maple Silestone helps the richly grained walnut top of the island stand out. "The idea is to treat the island like a piece of furniture," says architect Stuart Sampley. "In older homes, an island was a piece of furniture, so it would have had a top that was different from the perimeter." The Blanco Maple Silestone contains clear terrazzo chips that tend to take on the surrounding color, allowing it to blend in even more.

kitchen's identity. Particularly when several surfaces are involved, it pays to be aware that materials convey a character that may be at odds with the rest of the kitchen.

"We look for the kitchen to be consistent in design and detailing, and this definitely includes our choice of countertop materials," says designer Rafe Churchill of Sharon, Conn. "A contemporary kitchen can begin to lean traditional if the wrong material is used, and likewise, a traditional kitchen can even more easily move toward contemporary with a very cold and glossy countertop." For the traditional kitchens he designs, Churchill likes to use materials such as Danby and Carrara marbles, as well as Pietra Cardosa, soapstone, zinc, and wood.

These natural materials, wood in particular, exert a subconscious attraction that invites lingering. This makes them especially appropriate for gathering places. Architect Nicole Starnes Taylor uses wood for the "perch spaces" in the small Seattle kitchens she remodels. The attraction of the wood surface draws visitors out of the cook's zone and "helps define where you hang out," she says.

Achieving Balance through Contrast

With exotic choices abounding these days, homeowners often latch onto a unique countertop that can be difficult to pair with another, notes Courtney Fadness, who designed interiors for Massachusetts-based Hutker Architects. Getting two materials to coexist peacefully, she says, starts with establishing a hierarchy, and then a balance, between them. "You have to consider which one takes center stage and why it's taking center stage," Fadness says. "Then you figure out how to balance that or, alternatively, create contrast."

Breaking down materials into contrasting tonal groups—one for the kitchen's perimeter, another for the island—simplifies the process. You might, Fadness suggests, assign dark tones to the perimeter and contrast that with an island topped with light, veined marble. Austin, Texas, architect Cindy Black, whose firm, Hello Kitchen, focuses on kitchen design, also emphasizes using tonal qualities to strike the right balance. "We don't start with colors; we start with tones," Black says, adding that she then weighs material options based on durability, cost, and other qualities.

Countertop colors are influenced by the rest of the kitchen as well. When architect Stuart Sampley remodeled a midcentury home in Austin, the countertop options were narrowed significantly by the clients' selection of bright-orange perimeter cabinets. "It's such a bold color, you want to keep the rest of the palette black and white," he says. To provide contrast without competition, he chose black Silestone to top the white island, and white Silestone over the boldly colored perimeter cabinets. He uses these and similar materials when he wants a countertop to fade into the background. "They're not designed to make a statement," he explains. "They're designed to be durable and quiet."

With different materials, contrast can be used to balance one against the other. Says Churchill, "We like to use contrasting materials to minimize the coldness that stone can often introduce even to a traditional kitchen." Wood, he notes, "is very effective in warming up the room and introducing some texture and organic colors."

For Fadness and others, choosing more than one countertop surface is frequently a result of balancing clients' aesthetic preferences with their lifestyle and budget. "Budget is a big factor," she says. "A client might really want marble, but then it evolves into a conversation about whether there is a smaller area—a bar, for example—where we could have that material and still stay within our budget."

Alternative materials can help to maintain lifestyle sanity as well. Fadness recalls another client mesmerized by marble. "She loved the natural surface and the dramatic veining and the light color," Fadness says. "But she was concerned about the maintenance and durability. In that case, we did a beautiful center island as a showpiece with a huge slab of marble. We paired it with a coordinating Caesarstone® for the cooking area that pulled out the gray veining in the marble." When clients latch onto a specific aesthetic or trend, Fadness says, returning to issues of budget and lifestyle can help to determine which materials—or how much of each material—to use.

A Few Don'ts

Choosing countertops that harmonize is more an art than a science, but there are some mixes that raise a red flag. The first is that multiple materials typically don't work well in a very small kitchen. Likewise, it's usually a bad idea to use two materials that both exhibit strong patterns. Finally, pairing fakes with natural materials is risky. "Mixing natural materials with man-made surfaces would be visually confusing, much like having different finishes on cabinet hinges and nearby knobs," says Churchill. Black agrees: "I wouldn't mix something that's faux with a countertop that's the real version of the faux."

When the two materials have markedly different characteristics, however, it can work. "Marbles and granites that have a lot of movement pair nicely with quieter materials like Caesarstone that are dark gray or black and that have a little depth," says Fadness. It gets back to maintaining hierarchy and contrast. For the best guarantee of a good match, Fadness advises taking a step back when the choices become overwhelming. "I think it's important to have a strong concept from the beginning, and to let that original concept aid you in evaluating what countertop materials will work and which won't," she says. "You have to keep tying it back to concept and function, function, function. You can't do it all."

SOURCES

TERAGREN®
Bamboo
www.teragren.com

BROOKS CUSTOM
Walnut, maple, zinc
www.brookscustom.com

SPECIALTYSTAINLESS.COM
Stainless (antique matte)
www.specialtystainless.com

STONE SOURCE
Thassos marble
www.stonesource.com

SILESTONE
www.silestoneusa.com

**TORTORA MARBLE &
TILE DESIGN CENTER**
Granite and Cararra marble
www.nystone.houzz.com

A SURFACE FOR EVERY PURPOSE

WORKSURFACES: IT ALL DEPENDS
The best surface for a prep area depends on whether you're cutting, rolling, or assembling. Even then, preferences vary. "It really hinges on how the client is going to use the kitchen," says Nicole Starnes Taylor. "I think Carrara is a great worksurface, especially for rolling dough and baking." Rafe Churchill likes wood for working countertops, but he concedes that zinc is also "a great material and with time can show a beautiful patina."

Maple butcher block

Cararra marble

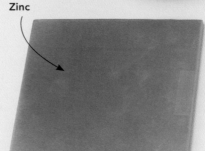

Zinc

Stainless steel

Walnut

Stranded bamboo

Silestone, Tao

Thassos marble

Juparana Pearl granite

SINK AREAS: MAKE IT WATERPROOF

Where water comes into play, easy maintenance and durability rule. When a client chose edge-grain white oak for her countertops, Cindy Black mounted the faucet in a slab of Thassos marble to keep water and wood separated. Rafe Churchill, whose traditional designs tend toward natural materials, also uses natural stones beside the sink, often with an integral drain board. Stainless steel, solid surfaces, and engineered stones—Zodiaq®, Silestone, Caesarstone, or Cambria®—also get the thumbs-up here.

GATHERING SPOTS: WOOD WINS

Wood is soft to the touch and beautiful to the eyes. As humans, we connect to it, making it a great surface for drawing people together. Natural stones, even granite, can have a similar allure, says Courtney Fadness: "When we bring those materials inside, we feel connected to them. Subconsciously, we feel comfortable with them."

A Bolder Backsplash

BY ANATOLE BURKIN

For a sleek, contemporary look in kitchens and bathrooms, back-painted glass has become a popular alternative to tile or synthetic solid-surface materials. The appeal is easy to understand: Back-painted glass is available in practically any color, is easy to clean, is durable, and can cover large surfaces without seams or grout lines. Best of all, its subtle, reflective surface brings a dramatic splash to any room.

Back-painted glass costs more than midrange ceramic tile but is on par with upper-end materials once all costs are figured. The biggest downside is availability: Not all small glass companies handle it. You'll likely have to find a large glass company, and you'll have more companies to choose from in larger metropolitan areas. Additionally, the substrate, usually drywall, must be absolutely flat in order for the glass to be installed securely.

What Is Back-Painted Glass?

The process of painting glass goes back to the 1950s, but it was less than 10 years ago that the material became popular in residential and commercial design, primarily for backsplashes and walls but also for countertops and even tabletops.

The glass used has to have a low iron content and so have only a minimal green tint. The paint, unique for this application, is typically applied in two layers, with an additional sealer coat applied to the back side of the glass at a special facility. Then the glass is baked to harden the coatings.

The glass used may be regular (polished surface), matte, sandblasted, or etched with a pattern. Size limits depend on the vendor you are working with, but standard sheets measuring 84 in. by 130 in. are common. That makes it possible to do an average bath surround with just three pieces of glass.

Back-painted glass, which is typically tempered, is available in thicknesses ranging from $\frac{1}{8}$ in. to 1 in. Thickness varies by application, but $\frac{1}{4}$ in. is typical for backsplashes. The glass can be drilled, notched, or even bent to suit many architectural situations.

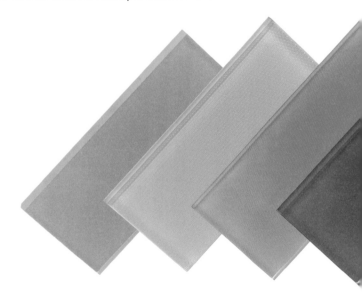

A CLEAN, MODERN LOOK.
This lavender backsplash
provides a pop of color
and an easy-to-clean sur-
face behind the cooktop.
Larger glass shops can
supply and install back-
painted glass.

Pricing varies based on thickness, cutouts, and other factors, but figure on about $60 per sq. ft. for ¼-in.-thick tempered glass. While that may seem high, the installation, assuming a flat wall, takes very little time compared to tile, which requires lots of cutting, setting, and grouting.

Where Can You Use It?

Kitchens and bathrooms are the most common places to install back-painted glass, but that's just a start. Architect Liesl Geiger-Kincade, who operates Studio Geiger Architecture in New York City, has used back-painted glass for 10 years for kitchen backsplashes, as tub surrounds in bathrooms, and even on the doors of an armoire cabinet. She loves how the material transforms a room. "Back-painted glass adds an ephemeral layer of light to a room," she says. "It is a continuously changing surface. Sometimes the surface is color, sometimes glowing light, sometimes reflection."

Geiger-Kincade has a suggestion for working with back-painted glass: "To get the color you'd like, be sure to ask for some samples. You need to specify the exact type and brand of glass you will use in order to control the color of the final installation. Typically, we ask for samples on regular glass and low-iron glass such as Starphire. Regular glass has green in it, and Starphire® is more clear, but it can also have a blue edge."

Designer Yana Mlynash of Mountain View, Calif., started using back-painted glass in 2009. "It's a reflective surface, which is great when you want to bring extra light into a room," she says. "The endless choice of colors is another benefit. You can do white cabinets and go bold on the glass color, allowing you to safely step away from the sterile, all-white look. And glass is very easy to keep clean."

Surface Requirements

A flat wall is imperative for installing back-painted glass, says Mark Manning, president of Farallon Construction in the San Francisco Bay Area.

TANGERINE DREAM. This kitchen island and backsplash highlight the jaw-dropping colors available on back-painted glass. Available in panels up to 84 in. by 130 in., the huge expanses of glass provide an uncluttered, seamless surface that's easy to clean.

LIGHT UP A SPACE. The reflective quality of back-painted glass makes it useful for drawing light into otherwise dark spaces. This kitchen's painted-glass north wall reflects light coming from windows on the opposite side of the room.

GROUT FREE. This white shower and adjacent wall show off the ultrasmooth surface achievable with back-painted glass. The seams where panels join are sealed with neutral-cure clear silicone, which doesn't attack the paint on the back side.

Manning prepares a wall of ½-in. or ⅝-in. drywall with a standard water-based primer. He checks the wall for flatness with a straightedge or a stringline, and if a stud is proud, he cuts away a section of drywall and planes down the hump. He also checks for drywall screws and nails left proud of the finished surface, which could scratch the paint on the back side of the glass.

Installation

Once fixtures, counters, and cabinets are placed, accurate measurements can be taken for glass backsplashes and walls. Robert Olson of Golden West Glass in Sonoma, Calif., has installed custom back-painted glass features in California's wine country for years. "Measurements are critical," he says. "We use lasers and levels to measure for flatness, check the substrate, and determine how we're controlling our shear and tip, the two ways glass can fall." Outlets and other obstacles should be in their final locations, or at least laid out accurately. In the case of a backsplash or wall, the glass rests on a counter or floor, what's called "going down hard." A ¹⁄₃₂-in.-thick sliver of clear plastic, called a block, is laid as a buffer along the bottom edge. The glass is attached directly to the wall using neutral-cure clear silicone, which doesn't react with the paint. J-channel provides extra holding capacity if that's necessary.

When a glass project requires multiple pieces, adjoining sheets are butt joined with a gap of ¹⁄₃₂ in. This allows for some wall movement without risking glass edges rubbing against and chipping each other. Joints are left alone in dry locations; in wet installations, the gap is sealed with neutral-cure clear silicone. The same is true of corner joints. Regarding maintenance, Olson says that soap and water are best. Glass cleaners containing ammonia can damage the painted surface by seeping through unsealed joints.

Kitchens Illuminated

BY JEFFREY R. DROSS

We used to light kitchens with one fixture placed in the middle of the ceiling, an arrangement that rarely provided enough light in the right location and often made kitchens stark, gloomy places. Unfortunately, the trend today toward recessed-can lighting has not improved the situation. Often improperly placed and poorly chosen, recessed cans cast inopportune shadows and create undesirable washes of glare that make it almost impossible to see what you're cutting on the counter, even with the added benefit of undercounter lighting. The truth is that despite opulent fixtures, cans by the dozen, and undercabinet lights, many of the lighting layouts that I see today are ineffective because designers chose the wrong fixtures and didn't optimize their placement.

If, however, you follow a few simple steps that help you properly position those cans and choose the right lamps to put in them, your kitchens will suddenly seem bigger, look brilliant, and function beautifully.

The Foundation Layer

Good lighting consists of three basic layers: ambient (general) lighting, accent (decorative) lighting, and task (work) lighting. Strategically linking these layers creates a cohesive design that takes the place of that single light source of the past.

Like a basic coat of paint, ambient light serves as a backdrop for all other light. By itself, it may not be interesting, but it serves the total design and the visual comfort of the end user. In today's kitchens, ambient light is provided primarily by recessed cans (see the photo on pp. 32–33). Unfortunately, it's in this initial ambient-lighting layer that most designers make their most egregious mistakes. Understanding how light is emitted from recessed fixtures is essential for positioning them correctly.

Beam Angle Is the Key to Spacing Cans

Unlike surface-mounted fixtures, which emit light 360° around, light emitted from recessed fixtures forms a parabolic or cone-shaped beam. This is why they are also colloquially called *downlights*. Think of recessed cans as automobile headlights installed upside down on the ceiling.

The shape of the cone of light is determined by a reflector that focuses the light into a specific beam angle. This reflector may be part of the fixture itself, or it may be built into the lamp (bulb). The "R" found in the popular bulb designations "R,"

"MR," and "PAR" indicates that these lamps have reflectors. In either case, whether built into the fixture or the bulb, you will find the beam angle specified by the manufacturer, generally on the box. This angle ranges from an extremely narrow 8° to a very wide 55°.

A narrow beam angle pushes all of the light into a slender cone, resulting in an intense quantity of light in a tiny space appropriate for illuminating a small worksurface, such as a cutting board or a sink. Wider beams take that same amount of light and disperse it over a broader area, which is generally more appropriate to ambient lighting. When using wide beam angles for ambient lighting, however, remember that the wider the beam, the lower the light intensity. To end up with an even distribution of the right amount of light, the quantity of fixtures and their beam angle must work in tandem so that beams overlap to cast even lighting, and beams don't intersect upper cabinets to create shadows on worksurfaces (see p. 34).

(see p. 34)

LIGHT LAYERING involves using several types of light in one room to serve different purposes. The basic layers are: (1) ambient lighting, (2) task lighting, and (3) accent or decorative lighting.

When calculating ambient lighting for a kitchen, lighting designers take most of their lighting measurements at countertop level. It's the place where eyes generally focus when in the kitchen. The first rule of recessed-light placement is that cans must be positioned so that the beam angle will just miss the lower lip of the upper cabinets. If your light beam touches the front surface of the upper cabinets, it will cast an unfortunate shadow on the countertop worksurface below.

SPACE LIGHTS USING BEAM ANGLE

BEAM ANGLE REFERS TO the angle at which light radiates from a lamp. The narrower the beam, the more intense the light. Narrow beam angles often are used for highlighting objects; wider beam angles are used for general illumination. Pay attention to the beam angle of overhead lights to eliminate glare and shadows in the kitchen. Wide-beam lights placed too close to cabinets create glare on the doors and shadows underneath. Improper placement of undercounter task lighting compounds this problem. Well-placed lighting positions the beam angle so that it misses the cabinet front, illuminating the countertop area and overlapping adjacent lights to produce solid overall illumination. Undercounter lights placed toward the front of the cabinets provide supplemental task lighting.

POOR PLACEMENT

GOOD PLACEMENT

Beam angles
should converge
about 6 in. above
countertop level.

Plotting It on Paper

To position cans correctly, find the beam angle of your lights, which is listed on the fixture, the manufacturer's website, the packaging, or the lamp itself. On your kitchen section drawing (a side view of the kitchen showing cabinets), use a protractor to plot the beam angle you want to use (40° is a good place to start, although you may find you need to adjust this later). Plot the beam's path relative to your upper cabinets, placing the first row of cans so that the beam angle just misses the front edge of the upper cabinet. To pinpoint the perpendicular placement of the next can along this first row, use the protractor again, this time on an elevation drawing (front view of the cabinets). Find a point 6 in. above the worksurface, and intersect the first beam angle with the second. Working backward, place the second can where that beam angle hits the ceiling. Using the protractor and beam-angle method, place the remainder of the cans.

Following this simple method will help you to avoid the most basic and most frequent mistakes I see in kitchen lighting.

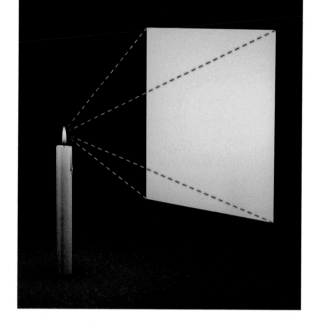

A FOOTCANDLE is a measurement of light intensity that represents the illumination of an average candle at a distance of 1 ft. from the surface being lit. Although largely abandoned abroad, footcandles (fc) are still used in the United States to express how much light is needed for a particular application, such as IES's recommended 30 fc for ambient lighting in an average kitchen.

WHY NOT LUMENS?

A LUMEN REPRESENTS HOW MUCH LIGHT a lamp emits. Since the introduction of super-energy-efficient lighting, lumens have largely replaced watts as the go-to measurement for lamp intensity. As a result, it's the number you'll find on most lamp packaging (indoor lamps typically have light outputs ranging from 50 to 10,000 lumens). The number of lumens, however, does not take into account the intensity of the light at any one point in the beam. That is why professionals gauge the illumination power of focused lights (such as can lights) in candlepower rather than lumens.

Calculating the Light Requirements

Once you've created a layout based on beam angle, you still have some work to do. The next step is determining how strong the lamps in your cans need to be to illuminate the space properly. The Illuminating Engineering Society (IES) recommends a minimum of 30 footcandles (fc) for general ambient lighting in a kitchen. This means you'll want an even distribution of 30 fc at countertop height.

This is an adequate amount of light for most kitchens. In some situations, however, more lighting might be needed. For example, if occupants are age 55 or older, the base recommendation from IES jumps to 40 fc. Someone with very poor vision may need much more. Young folks with excellent eyesight may get along with less, but stick to 30 fc as a starting point.

A footcandle is based on the output of one standard candle, burning 1 ft. away from the surface it illuminates. The other measure I use in lighting calculations is candlepower, which represents the traveling power of light emitted from a lamp.

These two measurements are the basis for the formulas I use to figure out how much light is needed at point A (the fixture) to see clearly at point B (countertop height).

Adjusting to the Situation

To complete our calculations, we have two more factors to take into account: room reflectance (how much of the lamp's light is absorbed or reflected) and ceiling height (the distance light has to travel to get to the countertop-height sweet spot).

A dark room absorbs light, requiring additional illumination. A kitchen finished with light colors requires less light. Because they become nonreflective black rectangles at night, windows increase lighting needs. Countertop materials factor into reflectance as well: Black-granite countertops may be beautiful, but they do not reflect much light.

To deal with these variables, IES recommends adjustment factors that can be applied to the base recommendation (30 fc) to ensure proper illumination. You can see an example at right of how I would apply these adjustments to a typical kitchen.

LIGHTING BY THE NUMBERS

GETTING AMBIENT LIGHT RIGHT REQUIRES calculations based on real-world conditions. To demonstrate, let's look at the kitchen pictured on pp. 32–33. This kitchen has an 8-ft. ceiling, and a floor and cabinets in midtone woods. The ceiling is white, and one wall is dark green. We'll assume the occupant is 58 years old. Here's how to calculate the ambient lighting needed for that room.

1. PLAN FOR CANS

With a protractor, mark your chosen beam angle on a section drawing so that the beams from the first row of cans miss the cabinets and intersect just above countertop height. To place adjacent cans, repeat the process on an elevation or plan view, maintaining the same overlap. (See the drawings at right.)

2. CALCULATE OVERALL AMBIENT-LIGHT NEEDS

Adjust ambient-light needs based on occupant age and room reflectance. IES adjustments are shown in charts 1 and 2, at right.

30 fc	Start with IES-recommended level of 30 fc.
30 fc x 1.33 = 39.9 fc	Multiply by age factor of 1.33 because the homeowner is 58 years old (see chart 1).
39.9 fc x 1 = 39.9 fc	Multiply by room reflectance factor of 1 because the wall, ceiling, and floor colors are of medium colorations (see charts 1 and 2).
39.9 fc x 1.33 = 53.07 fc	Multiply by countertop background factor of 1.33 because the countertops are dark (see chart 1).

Total footcandles required: 53.07. We can round to 53 before proceeding to the next step.

3. CALCULATE REQUIRED CANDLEPOWER

Based on the footcandle requirements established in step 2, we now factor in the ceiling height to arrive at the candlepower required for each fixture.

$cp = D^2 \times fc$	Start with the inverse-square law.
$cp = 25 \times 53$	The room has 8-ft. ceilings, so the worksurface is 5 ft. away; 5 x 5 = 25. We know the required fc is 53 from our calculations in step 2.
$cp = 1325$	Each recessed can must provide a candlepower of at least 1325 to illuminate the room adequately.

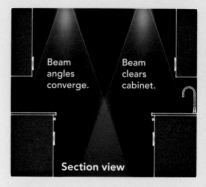

Beam angles converge.

Beam clears cabinet.

Section view

A SECTION VIEW (ABOVE) allows you to correctly position the cans relative to the cabinets. An elevation (frontal) view or a plan view (right) then can be used to space cans in each row for full illumination.

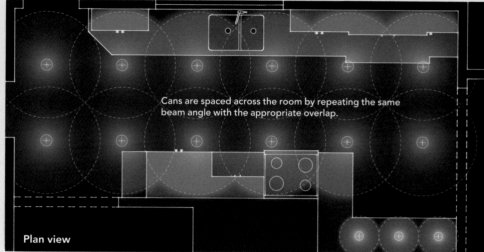

Cans are spaced across the room by repeating the same beam angle with the appropriate overlap.

Plan view

CHART 1

ADJUSTMENT FACTORS FOR FOOTCANDLE LEVELS

Adjustment factor	0.66	1.0	1.33
Age	Under 40	40–55	Over 55
Average room reflectance (ceiling, walls, and floor)	Light (over 70%)	Medium (30%–70%)	Dark (under 30%)
Task background reflectance (countertop color)	Light (over 70%)	Medium (30%–70%)	Dark (under 30%)

4. FIND FIXTURES

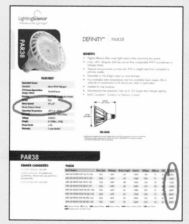

Match candlepower needs to a lamp or fixture with the right beam spread and candlepower. This information can be found on the manufacturers' spec sheets, websites, and catalogs. A little more candlepower is better than not enough.

For more calculations, check out *Kitchen and Bath Lighting Made Easy* by Michael DeLuca (National Kitchen & Bath Association, 2001).

CHART 2

CALCULATING ROOM REFLECTANCE*

WALL OR CEILING COLORS	REFLECTANCE (%)
White, light cream	70–80
Light yellow	55–65
Light green, pink	45–50
Light blue, light gray	40–45
Beige, ocher, light brown, olive green	25–35
Orange, vermilion, medium gray	20–25
Dark colors (green, blue, red, gray)	10–15

MATERIALS	REFLECTANCE (%)
White plaster	80
White tile	65–75
Limestone	35–70
Marble	30–70
Sandstone	20–40
Granite	20–25
Gray concrete	15–40
Brick	10–20
Carbon/black	2–10
Mirror	95
Clear glass	6–8
Maple	60
Birch	35–50
Oak (light)	25–35
Cherry	15–30
Oak (dark)	10–15
Mahogany	6–12
Walnut	5–10
Tin	67–72
Stainless	50–60
Aluminum	55–58

*If unknown, assume medium (30%–70%).

After these adjustments are made, one last formula is needed to determine the amount of light required from your fixtures. That's because a lamp placed 18 in. from a surface delivers a lot more light than the same lamp located 8 ft. away. To calculate how much candlepower a lamp must produce to get the required illumination where it's needed, lighting designers use the inverse-square law. According to this rule, the candlepower (cp) of your fixture should be equal to the distance from the light source to the countertop area squared (D^2) and then multiplied by the footcandles required. The equation is written $cp = D^2 \times fc$. The example on p. 36 demonstrates this formula for an 8-ft. ceiling.

Just a reminder: I've been measuring light needs at countertop height, but I'm focusing only on ambient light. For countertop tasks, you'll want to supplement this 30 fc of ambient light with another 40 fc or more of undercabinet lighting to reach the 70 fc recommended for worksurfaces.

Ceiling height makes a significant difference in the amount of illumination required to light a kitchen properly. If the ceiling height is just 2 ft. taller (10 ft.), you need almost twice as much illumination to deliver an adequate amount of light to that countertop sweet spot.

Now Find Your Lights . . . or Maybe Start Over

After you've established the location of your cans and calculated the beam angle and candlepower, you need to select the right lamps. Invariably, after looking through manufacturers' catalogs and websites, or receiving help from a lighting consultant, you'll seek out the product that emits the requisite candlepower combined with the beam angle you used in your lighting layout, only to discover that this lamp or integrated fixture does not exist.

So it's back to the drawing board for some recalculation. For example, if you planned the spacing based on a wide beam spread and the ceilings are very high, you may not find a lamp that can deliver the required amount of light. You may need to lay out the cans again and add more fixtures, using a tighter beam angle. Remember, fixtures that have a smaller beam angle deliver a larger concentration of light. Or you may opt to use fixtures that hang from the ceiling, effectively lowering the level of your light source.

You also may discover that you cannot place those cans in the ideal location because of a stray joist or other obstruction that sits in the middle of your perfect layout. I encountered this problem in my own kitchen. To provide the right amount of light on my counters, I sacrificed the amount of light at the center of the room. If a kitchen does not include an island, this is a good place for less light. I made the necessary adjustments in can placement to accommodate my joists, favoring worksurfaces and de-emphasizing perfect light in the center of the room. These kinds of adjustments are always a judgment call. Use logic and common sense, and you'll like the results.

Photos have been edited for illustrative purposes.

PART 2

Fixtures and Materials

Undercabinet Lighting

BY DEBRA JUDGE SILBER

There may be no place where advances in home lighting are more apparent than under kitchen cabinets. White-hot halogens and temperamental fluorescents are making way for a new crop of LEDs that are not just super-efficient—they're as aesthetically pleasing as the long-dominant incandescent. "Undercabinet lighting is one of the areas where LED is really ideal," says Joe Rey-Barreau, an architect and spokesman for the American Lighting Association who teaches at the University of Kentucky's College of Design. "There's nothing else I would even vaguely recommend." Improvements in color rendering, color temperature, and longevity are behind LEDs' seemingly universal acceptance by lighting designers. Their energy efficiency is remarkable, and they provide more lumens per watt than incandescent bulbs (or lamps, as they're called in the industry). Their life of 50,000 or more hours makes lamp replacement obsolete. Instead, in the case of many LED products, the presumption is that the fixture itself will be replaced after 15 to 20 years with a better and presumably less expensive version.

For all their benefits, high-quality LEDs remain expensive, in part due to the phosphor coatings used to enhance the quality of their light. Until that changes, alternatives such as xenon, halogen, and

FLUORESCENT. With modest improvement in color rendering, ⅝-in.-dia. T5 tubes remain an economical under-cabinet option.

HALOGEN. A reputation for burning hot and having a relatively short life compared to other lamps cost halogens their popularity.

XENON. Low-voltage xenon lamps offer warm (not hot) operation, last about 10,000 hours, and provide adequate light at a moderate price.

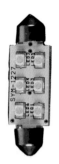

LED. Forget that blinding blue light. Today's long-lasting LEDs offer variable color tempera-tures and are vastly more efficient than incandescents.

even fluorescent lamps will continue to be used in undercabinet fixtures.

This emphasis on the light source has over-shadowed what used to be the decision in choosing undercabinet lighting: the fixture. Still, this choice remains important. Different types of fixtures not only install differently, but they cast light differently and create different architectural effects. This combination of light source and fixture has complicated the undercabinet-lighting decision.

Remember What It's There For

Make no mistake when specifying undercabinet fixtures: The primary reason to have light shining on your countertop is to aid in food preparation. In the practice known as light layering—that is, illuminating a space using different types of light with different functions—this is called task lighting. Because undercabinet lighting often plays a secondary role in accenting a backsplash or providing subtle illumination after hours (especially when dimmed), it's often regarded as accent lighting. This misconception can lead to choosing undercabinet lighting that does not provide enough illumination for countertop work.

With that understanding, the next step is to con-sider how the kitchen is used and who its occupants are. Jeffrey R. Dross, director for education and industry trends at Kichler® Lighting, points out that older occupants want more illumi-nation in the task area, as do avid cooks. "If you do a lot of home cooking, you're going to want more light than someone who uses the countertop to look at the Yellow Pages for carryout," he says.

Color Temperature Matters

Other factors to consider are the surfaces and style of the kitchen. The color temperature of the lamps you choose will determine whether your undercabinet lighting evokes a warm, traditional feel or a bright, modern one. Color temperature also impacts how food appears—worth remembering if you use your countertop for an impromptu buffet.

Color temperature is measured in kelvins (K). Residential lamps typically have a color temperature that ranges from about 2700K (the light cast from an old-fashioned incandescent) to 5000K (the color of daylight). The higher the color temperature, the harsher and "colder" the light. In North America, where incandescent lighting has been the rule, designers tend to recommend warmer temperatures, edging a bit higher for contemporary kitchens. "The color of the light should match the color of the environment," says Dross, who recommends 2700K lamps for wood-tone kitchens and 3000K for white or steel kitchens.

One reason the new LEDs have taken under-cabinet culture by storm is that manufacturers have discovered how to tame the cold, blue light of the LED with phosphor coatings that cast a warm, pleasant light. San Francisco-based lighting designer Randall Whitehead especially likes new LEDs that

COLOR TEMPERATURE: HOW WE SEE FOOD— AND EVERYTHING ELSE

WHETHER YOUR CHICKEN SOUP APPEARS golden yellow or simply pale may be a reflection of your cooking skills—or it may depend on the light source you're viewing it under. Old-school fluorescents—and more recently, inexpensive LEDs—had a reputation for casting an unflattering light on people and some foods because of their high (5000K) color temperature. This has all changed with the new generation of lamps, which offer a wide range of color temperatures. The difference can be seen in these apples photographed under LED lights of different color temperatures. While cool, crisp light enhances the green of the apple, warmer light brightens the wooden base.

5000K

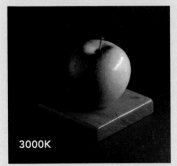
3000K

2400K

WARM LIGHT IN A WHITE KITCHEN. Architect Eric Gjerde from Essex, Mass., chose LED lighting with a color temperature of 3200K for this kitchen remodel.

allow homeowners a range of temperatures. "This allows you to have a cooler color to show off your modern kitchen and a warmer color to show off your buffet," he says.

Color temperatures for halogens and xenons hover around 3000K. While large fluorescents are available in many color temperatures, Rey-Barreau points out that the smaller T5 tubes used in undercabinet fixtures haven't quite got the range. "For undercabinet lighting, it's hard to get fluorescent bulbs that have good color," he says.

In addition to temperature, you should look for a high color-rendering index (CRI) for your undercabinet lighting. CRI represents how well

light interprets color and is rated on a sale of 0 to 100, with 100 being the best. Undercabinet lighting should have a minimum CRI of 85; for LEDs, Whitehead recommends 90. In general, the higher the CRI, the more expensive the lamp. If you can't find the CRI listed in the product literature of a lamp, don't buy it, Dross says.

The Right Light in the Right Place

The best task lighting puts light where you need it. Experts recommend placing undercabinet light sources toward the front of the cabinet, where they can illuminate the section of countertop where most prep work takes place. They shy away from direct-

(continued on p. 46)

WHAT'S GOING UNDER CABINETS NOW

WITH IMPROVEMENTS IN BOTH LAMPS and the fixtures that house them, there have never been more choices in undercabinet lighting. Here are some popular options.

LED TAPE: OUTPUT IS EVERYTHING

LED tapes are all the rage, but most are better as accent lighting —under toe kicks or coves—than undercabinet task lights. Some manufacturers, however, have introduced high-output tapes that provide satisfactory undercabinet light. These include Maxim® Lighting's Ultima Star 24v (center right) with an output of 254 lumens per ft., more than twice the 77-lumen output of its Basic tape (near right). Both have a set color temperature of 3500K. The Color Flex tape (far right) ups the ante with a color temperature that adjusts from 2900K to 5000K. The key to getting a good LED tape is to test the product at a reputable lighting showroom that deals with established manufacturers. Complaints include adhesive failure and finicky connections, particularly among the many low-quality imports on the market.

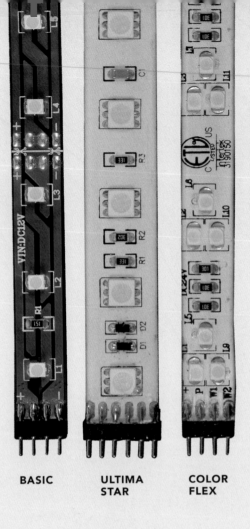

BASIC **ULTIMA STAR** **COLOR FLEX**

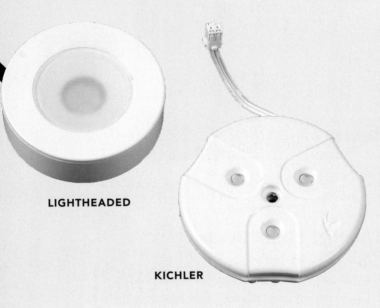

LIGHTHEADED

KICHLER

PUCKS: IMPROVING A SPOTTY REPUTATION

Once-standard halogen and xenon puck lights are rapidly being pushed aside by LED versions, which not only are highly energy efficient but run much cooler. (Halogen pucks have been known to melt items stored in cabinets above them.) Some are so thin they're barely noticeable even under flat-bottomed European-style cabinets, such as Kichler's LED disk (near left). Lightheaded™'s puck (far left), challenges the warm cast of incandescents with a color temperature of 2700K. Regardless of lamping, pucks, disks, and buttons intended for undercabinet tasks should be weighed carefully with regard to beam spread and intensity to ensure sufficient illumination on the countertop. While some designers like the rhythmic pattern pucks produce under a cabinet, others dislike the spots of light or feel they interfere with functionality.

LOW-VOLTAGE MODULAR: CHOOSE YOUR LOCATION AND YOUR LAMP

Low-voltage modular lighting is the undercabinet choice for many designers because fixtures can be mounted toward the front of the cabinets, where they deliver the most light. Modular LED units can be exceptionally slim but costly, which has allowed modulars outfitted with incandescent (typically xenon) lamps to remain popular. The 12v, 18w xenon lamps used in the Kichler model at right have a color temperature of 2700K and a CRI of 100, but their efficacy of 6 lumens per watt can't match the 41 lumens per watt of their LED counterpart (far right).

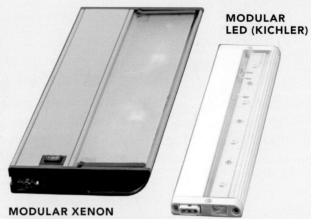

MODULAR LED (KICHLER)

MODULAR XENON (KICHLER)

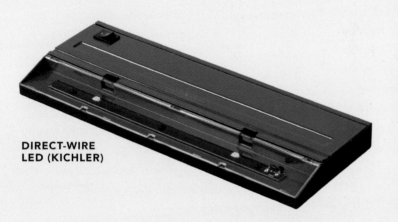

DIRECT-WIRE LED (KICHLER)

DIRECT-WIRE LED: BETTER LIGHT IN AN IMPERFECT PLACE

Lighting designers typically caution against direct-wire undercabinet fixtures, because by necessity they're mounted against the backsplash—not near the cabinet front where their light is needed. But if the electrician has already stubbed out a line under each cabinet, or if you're hoping to upgrade the fluorescents you've had for years, direct-wire LED units may be the answer. A built-in driver steps down the current to power the LED chips.

REMOTE-PHOSPHOR LENS LEDS: BETTER YET

If LEDs have one remaining drawback, it's this: It takes multiple LEDs to light a countertop, and those tiny multiple points of light create annoying multiple shadows on the workspace (left). That's been eliminated in LED fixtures where the yellow phosphor coating required to create white light from blue LEDs is applied to the lens rather than the individual chips. Commanding the category is Tech Lighting®'s Unilume line, which includes both modular and light-bar type fixtures (right).

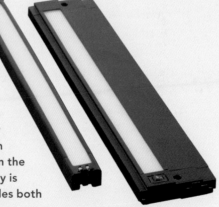

UNILUME LED (TECH LIGHTING)

wire fixtures, which, because they tap directly into 120v stub-outs beneath the cabinets, are mounted against the backsplash. (Some manufacturers make up for this by aiming the lamps forward, a situation that can leave the backsplash in shadow.) Though wired to a direct current, many direct-wire products have a built-in transformer allowing the use of brighter, longer-life 12v or 24v halogen or xenon lamps. On the plus side, direct-wire fixtures are generally inexpensive, and their installation is familiar to most electricians.

The better choice, designers say, is modular low-voltage fixtures that can be mounted in a forward position and linked together to create a continuous line of light across the worksurface. Typically more expensive than direct-wire options, they also require more planning to determine what type of transformer will be used and where it will be mounted. One light per cabinet is typically recommended to ensure adequate illumination across the countertop.

An opaque lens guards against one of the major crimes of undercabinet lights, particularly LEDs: the annoying dots of light and multiple shadows produced by multiple light sources. "A lot of LED products have a clear or stippled lens," observes Whitehead. "On a shiny countertop, you'll see the individual diodes. You want to make sure it has a frosted lens to diffuse the light."

Puck or disk lighting is a mixed bag. Disks can create dramatic dots of light on a backsplash—but that's not ideal if the goal is useful task lighting. Halogen pucks in particular are notorious for damaging foodstuffs stored above them with their intense heat. New LED versions eliminate that concern, and some offer a much thinner profile, not to mention longer life and more efficient operation.

For all their hype, LED tapes present challenges in undercabinet applications because the light they provide is often not bright enough. Some manufacturers offer LED tapes in several intensities, including super-bright tapes that provide just

enough power for adequate task lighting. Carefully chosen, these can work in applications where intensity is not a concern. Another option is to double up the tape for more light, but that means doubling the cost as well.

Trading Up Is Part of the Process

An important truth about LED tapes and most LED fixtures is that when the diodes die out, the entire unit, not the individual chips, will need to be replaced. This is a fundamental shift in lighting that few professionals and even fewer consumers have managed to get their heads around, says Rey-Barreau. Add to that the expense of LED lights and the rapid pace at which LED technology is progressing, and the potential for buyer's remorse becomes staggering.

Still, Rey-Barreau is upbeat. "The nice thing is that they have gotten to the point where the quality of the product and the efficacy is so good that even the thing you're stuck with is not bad," he says. "And 10 years from now, you'll replace it with a better product at a better price."

Ready-to-Assemble Kitchen Cabinets

BY ANATOLE BURKIN

Practically anything can be purchased online these days, and kitchen cabinets are no exception. Ready-to-assemble (RTA) cabinets cost 30% to 50% less than their assembled brethren. Ikea®, CabParts, The Home Depot®, TheRTAStore.com, and many other companies offer a huge selection of cabinet styles and ac-cessories that can be delivered flat-packed to your front door. They're pretty easy to assemble and only require a few basic tools.

CRISP AND CLEAN. Ikea is the best-known RTA cabinet brand. Its latest line, Sektion, includes hundreds of cabinets and accessories. The Järsta wall cabinets and Ringhult base cabinets (shown) have high-gloss fronts for easy cleaning.

CABPARTS

CABPARTS, in existence since 1987, mostly serves professional builders and remodelers (the website doesn't offer much in the way of design help), but Stuart Thompson, the company's general manager, says that CabParts will work with "high-functioning DIYers." He explains, "We don't mind helping people, but there is only so much we can do. We're not big, but we're mighty. We ship all over the United States and beyond." CabParts offers cabinet boxes in 1,500 standard sizes and makes custom sizes as well. Boxes are melamine-coated particleboard or plywood. Stock melamine offerings are white, almond, gray, black, and natural maple (wood-grain pattern). The company also carries red-oak, maple, and cherry (all unfinished) wood veneers on MDF, plus a prefinished maple plywood.

Cabinets are assembled with Confirmat screws and 8mm hardwood dowels for alignment, or 8mm by 30mm hardwood dowels that come preglued and that are wetted just before assembly. CabParts also offers a huge selection of drawers that can be ordered with or without cabinet boxes.

THUMBS-UP
Rock-solid Confirmat joinery and high-quality veneer-plywood construction.

THUMBS-DOWN
Plain-Jane slab fronts and doors; no printed instructions.

JOINERY. Preglued alignment dowels and Confirmat screws with predrilled holes; feels rock solid and comes with correct (EZP3) driver bit.

HARDWARE. Blum® undermount soft-close; slide-attachment clips come installed on drawer box; 100° Blum hinges.

CONSTRUCTION. ¾-in. prefinished maple-plywood box; ¼-in. prefinished maple-plywood back.

FINISH. High-quality clear finish over veneer plywood with corresponding edgebanding.

THE HOME DEPOT

THE HOME DEPOT offers two lines of RTA cabinets. The company's Eurostyle line, which is made in Canada, has a contemporary look with boxes made of melamine-coated particleboard in a handful of color options. Doors are available in several materials, including solid wood. Heartland Cabinetry is The Home Depot's entry-level line.

According to Michael Holden, the company's merchant for stock cabinets and countertops, "The Eurostyle cabinets are currently the most popular." Prices are competitive with those of Ikea's RTA cabinets. Cabinets are not stocked in stores and must be ordered online, although some stores allow you to order them in-house.

The Home Depot offers a design gallery and some online help via messaging as well as some in-store assistance. "We offer design services through our Design Connect team that supports store and online customers, but there are no online design tools at this time," says Holden.

THUMBS-UP
Very low price, with free shipping to home or local store.

THUMBS-DOWN
Metal drawer box rattles and is tough to adjust for proper reveal.

JOINERY. Screws with plastic toggle-like inserts; finished box feels rickety, and screw heads strip easily.

CONSTRUCTION. ¾-in. particleboard box; ³⁄₁₆-in. hardboard back.

HARDWARE. Metal drawer box with integral soft-close slides; tougher adjustments than with other styles; 100° hinges.

FINISH. Melamine-coated particleboard with stained solid-wood doors and drawer front.

IKEA

IKEA offers lots of door and drawer designs, including traditional frame-and-panel style with a number of profile options, simple Shaker style, and the more modern slab style. All of its cabinet components come prefinished. Door-material choices include melamine-coated particleboard or fiberboard, as well as veneered and solid wood. Prices start surprisingly low.

What makes Ikea unique is that you can go to a store and come home with a complete kitchen the same day, although not all products are available at all stores for immediate pickup. Placing an order for delivery direct to your home is a more convenient option. You'll get everything at once, and you won't have to bring a truck or trailer to the store.

THUMBS-UP
Sturdy Maximera drawer box with full-extension slides.

THUMBS-DOWN
Cabinet has many parts and comes in many separate boxes.

 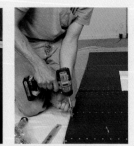

CONSTRUCTION. ¾-in. particleboard box with a ⅛-in. fiberboard back; steel reinforcement and hanging brackets.

HARDWARE. Maximera drawer box is sturdy and has full-extension soft-close slides; Forvara box is weaker and has three-quarter extension slides; 100° Blum hinges.

JOINERY. Cam locks like those found on other Ikea products; box assembles quickly but doesn't feel as strong as boxes assembled using other methods.

FINISH. Melamine-coated box with stained solid-wood door and drawer front.

THeRTAstore.com

THERTASTORE.COM, head-quartered in Hopewell Junction, N.Y., offers free design help and dozens of cabinet styles and sizes. Even the least expensive models have boxes made from ¼-in. hardwood plywood. The cabinets are pre-finished and assembled with either cam locks or sturdy and easy-to-use steel clips. Drawers have dovetailed joints and are generally shipped knocked down. They are assembled on-site with wood screws.

Somewhat unusual for RTA cabinets, many models from TheRTAStore.com have face frames, which provide greater flexibility when cabinets are installed on out-of-plumb walls. The face frames come fully assembled, with doors installed and hinges adjusted.

THUMBS-UP
Cabinet is easy to assemble and comes in a single box.

THUMBS-DOWN
Assembly instructions are basic and include no written steps.

HARDWARE. Undermount soft-close drawer slides; 100° hinges.

CONSTRUCTION. ¼-in. plywood box and ¼-in. plywood back.

JOINERY. Unique system with steel clips that join the panels for a fast and strong connection.

FINISH. Multilayer glaze with hand-applied pinstriping.

RTA FROM A DIYER

PLANNING AND INSTALLING A KITCHEN made from ready-to-assemble cabinets will take the average homeowner several weeks if not months.

Mark and Donna Eis of Walden, N.Y., tackled a kitchen remodel in late 2012. Mark considers himself an intermediate-to-advanced-level DIYer. The project involved gutting their 140-sq.-ft. kitchen and installing Ikea cabinets at $120 per lin. ft. (both uppers and lowers). Regarding the layout, Donna preferred graph paper and pencil to Ikea's online design tool, which she found cumbersome to use. "If you're doing the layout design yourself, spend extra time in the planning phase," she advises. "Make lists of your needs and preferences, and observe your family's habits, paying special attention to where your kitchen feels awkward or crowded. Mark out possible cabinet layouts in masking tape on existing cabinets, and walk through imaginary meal preparation and cleanup to get a sense of flow."

"Assembly and installation combined took about one to three hours per cabinet, depending on the complexity of the unit and the hardware," adds Mark. "As with most things, there was a learning curve. Once we got used to working with the cabinets and hardware, the process sped up."

Should I Buy RTA Cabinets?

How do you know if RTA cabinets are right for you? For starters, if you're not that handy and need a lot of help designing and installing your kitchen, you're probably better off working with a home center or kitchen showroom that offers design and installation services. This is because the price advantage of RTA cabinets decreases quickly if you have to factor in design, assembly, and installation.

If you're a professional contractor, consider what builder Mike Guertin says about using RTA cabinets in his business: "The assembly time kills it for professionals, except in the rare case where you need cabinets immediately in order to finish a job. Some RTAs are stocked and can be delivered in a few days versus several weeks for assembled cabinets."

The tradeoff for perhaps dozens of hours of work putting together a kitchen's worth of cabinets is at least a 30% savings in cost over assembled cabinets. Besides the assembly time, you'll also need a space to store and assemble the cabinets before you install them. Furthermore, you'll have to measure the job accurately and design the kitchen yourself, or pay extra for those services. Lisa Finnin-Ciccoli, a local marketing specialist with Ikea, says the most common mistakes beginners make involve measuring. "Exact measurements of wall placement, ceiling height, utility locations, and location and size of doors and windows are very important for planning and installation," she says.

Also important, she adds, is the time commitment: "Many DIYers underestimate how much time it takes to install their kitchen cabinets. A 10-ft. by 10-ft. kitchen can have over 100 different pieces, so organization is key. Make sure your measurements are correct, and inventory all your pieces. Group them together by cabinet to make sure you have everything you need."

Stuart Thompson, general manager of CabParts, has heard his share of complaints from DIYers.

"With wall cabinets, make sure that they are good and square, and that the back is attached firmly," he says. Regarding lower cabinets, he tells customers "to take pains to get the edges flush with one another and make sure the box is square." Doing so ensures that the door and drawer reveals are consistent.

Thompson likes building a platform for the boxes instead of using the leveling legs sold by many manufacturers. With the platform, he explains, "you level once, then install." That said, leg levelers work just as well, but they take more time. When it comes to choosing a joinery method, Thompson has a favorite: "I prefer Confirmat screws because the joint is held in tension, which makes the boxes stronger during handling."

Choosing a Supplier

Big companies such as Ikea and The Home Depot have retail stores where customers can see their products up close, and their design and ordering processes have been refined through many years of experience. Large online merchants such as TheRTAStore.com have catalogs of photos of their cabinets and also offer online design tools, often for free. They can arrange in-person design services, and assembly and installation are available for additional fees. Smaller RTA companies may not have all the online bells and whistles of their bigger competitors, but if you can handle a tape measure and a drill-driver, most of them can work with you online or by phone. If you have very specific needs— whether they be about sizing, wood selection, grain matching, or custom moldings—the smaller shops are your best bet.

If you're in a hurry, big companies have warehouses stocked with many of their products ready to ship. Small companies sometimes require four to six weeks to complete your order. One final thing to keep in mind is that many high-quality assembled cabinets are certified by the Kitchen Cabinet Manufacturers Association, an assurance that you're getting a quality product. Unfortunately, there is no industry certification for RTA cabinets because so much of the performance depends on the assembly. To protect yourself from shoddy products, review the information here, read online reviews, and look carefully at the warranties offered. Some are as long as 25 years.

Semicustom Cabinets

NENA DONOVAN LEVINE

If your kitchen cabinets are decades old and you're homing in on a renovation, consider this advice: "Ya gotta know the territory." It's from *The Music Man,* a show as old as those very cabinets. Dispensed by a traveling salesman headed for River City, it's also a great mantra to use when surveying today's kitchen-cabinetry landscape.

In 2012, the cost of an average kitchen renovation was over $47,000, according to a National Kitchen and Bath Association member survey. Cabinetry consumes one-third or more of that amount. You can do the math, but it is safe to say this investment deserves careful consideration.

There are three broad categories of kitchen cabinets: Stock cabinets tend to be the most affordable but offer the least variety of style and finishes, are sometimes made from lower-quality materials, and may be constructed for a shorter useful life. Custom cabinets are at the other extreme in that they can be made of familiar or exotic materials to any size, style, and quality. Semicustom cabinets fall between stock and custom cabinets and are arguably the best value. The Kitchen Cabinet Manufacturers Association defines semicustom as "built to order but within a defined set of construction parameters; available in standard widths but with more choices for depth and height modifications." According to one of the organization's recent member surveys, the semicustom category makes up 46% of the overall market.

MasterBrand® Cabinets has lines in all three categories. Stephanie Pierce, manager of MasterBrand's design studio, says that unlike the company's stock line—which is limited to very specific dimensions, styles, and finishes—its semicustom lines, including Diamond® and Decorá, offer designers and builders "flexibility within limitations." More specifically, these brands' offerings can be customized only to the degree of the shops' capabilities. At the custom end of the spectrum, Master Brand's Omega Cabinets will outsource any fabrication that its shop is not capable of.

Snapshot of a Giant Category

Semicustom cabinets are built upon receipt of an order, so lead time is longer than it would be for stock cabinets, which you can sometimes get off the shelf at a home center. It's shorter than it would be for custom cabinets, however, although this varies based on the complexity of the cabinets and the

SEMI-WHAT? Called semicustom, the category of cabinetry that makes up the lion's share of the market is full of variety. These cabinets, from Canyon Creek, are chocolate-antiqued creme color. The island is burnished ebony stain. Details like the crown molding and island legs are often standard features of semicustom lines.

FACE FRAMED, FRAME-LESS, OR BOTH? You don't have to choose. These cabinets from Canyon Creek offer a clean, frameless look with face frames hidden behind the door and drawer fronts. Some installers prefer this arrangement for durability and ease of installation.

builder's availability. Merillat®'s semicustom Classic line can ship in as little as five to ten days. Canyon Creek®'s Katana line has a lead time as short as four weeks from order to delivery. Certain upgrades can push lead times out to six weeks or more.

Semicustom cabinets are offered in standard 3-in.-wide increments from 9 in. to 45 in. For an upcharge, you can modify this to ⅛ in. Such precise dimensions reduce the call for filler strips and minimize wasted space. Standard cabinet depths and heights also can be increased or decreased for

PULLOUT PANTRY IS NARROW ENOUGH. Standard cabinet widths start at 9 in. and can be specified in 3-in. increments (or smaller for an upcharge). This pullout spice rack from Merillat is a great use of narrow space next to the oven and cooktop.

NO WASTED SPACE. This clever end-panel door from MasterBrand makes the most of a few unused inches for magazine storage and office supplies.

HARDWARE MATTERS. Most manufacturers offer hardware options to enhance storage in their cabinets. Some can be outfitted with aftermarket hardware as well. These Diamond cabinets have elegant and useful storage that keeps cookware from getting lost deep inside the island.

an upcharge. So if using a standard 24-in.-deep base cabinet doesn't allow adequate clearance in a pantry or a passageway, you can reduce the box depth and still use the particular cabinets you were hoping for. Standard wall cabinets are 30 in. and 36 in. tall, but sometimes 33 in. or even 42 in. works better with a particular ceiling height. Again, with most semicustom lines, this level of customization is possible.

Semicustom cabinets are available with face-frame or frameless construction or both. The choice is mostly aesthetic: Face frames are more common on traditional-style cabinets, and frameless cabinets are more contemporary looking. But there are plenty of exceptions.

On face-frame cabinets, the doors can be inset or they can be overlaid to reveal more or less of the frames. The hinges attach to the face frames.

Doors on frameless cabinets cover the cabinet box's finished front edge. Door hinges attach to the box sides. Frameless construction offers a more open interior and is typical of today's European cabinetry. In the United States, by contrast, face-frame construction outsells frameless, according to Danielle Mikesell, Merillat's director of marketing. Both traditional and frameless cabinets can be ordered with a panoply of door and drawer styles, wood species, finishes, crown-molding profiles, and box-construction options. Some manufacturers will even combine face-frame construction with a frameless aesthetic. When it comes to style and construction, most of what is commonly built by custom-cabinet shops can be found in semicustom cabinets.

Cabinet doors and shelves are typically ¾ in. thick. A loaded, ¾-in. shelf can span a 36-in.-wide

WHAT'S NOT SEMICUSTOM

THE DISTINCTION BETWEEN STOCK, SEMICUSTOM, and custom cabinets can be blurry. Some manufacturers, like Merillat, offer lines in more than one category. Here's a look at the alternatives to semicustom.

STOCK

"Stock" refers to cabinet inventory stocked—and sometimes stacked—at a manufacturer or retailer. Options for door style, wood species, finish, molding profile, and hardware are limited to what's there. Materials reflect a budget price point; for example, a stock cabinet door may be ½ in. thick, while a semicustom or custom door measures ¾ in. Cabinet-box size is limited to 3-in.-wide increments from 9 in. to 45 in. Depths for both wall and base cabinets are fixed, and warranties are the shortest on the market—often five years or less. Benefits of stock cabinetry include its entry-level price and fast (immediate or within a few days) delivery. Stock quality may suit a rental unit, starter house, or budget kitchen. Limited choices may inspire DIY creativity and yield excellent value.

CUSTOM

"Custom" cabinets, originating in a small shop or a large manufacturing facility, are built to client specifications upon receipt of the order. They can incorporate curved doors, complex angles, odd box sizes, and unusual colors. If you want to hand-select or book-match exotic veneers, you can. Options for door style, wood species, finish, crown-molding profile, box selection, accessories, and hardware are enormous. Benefits of custom cabinetry include vast choice, tailored fit and finish, and individualized fabrication. Expect a premium price tag and longer remodel time, since custom lead times run eight weeks to several months. Large manufacturers offer generous (even lifetime) warranties for custom products. Small-shop warranties vary. Custom implies top quality, but it's not a given from every small cabinet shop.

cabinet, while thinner shelves may bow across that span. Full-depth shelves, adjustable in ½-in. increments, maximize storage. For organizing cabinet interiors, there are plenty of accessories, such as roll-out shelves and lazy susans. Companies such as Häfele®, Knape & Vogt®, and Rev-A-Shelf® make bins, baskets, and recycling containers to complement semicustom lines.

Semicustom lines offer warranties that may equal the limited-lifetime warranty typical for custom cabinets. Canyon Creek, Merillat, and KraftMaid® all offer such warranties on some lines that cover the product for as long as the purchaser owns it, with certain exclusions. Unfinished products are excluded, for example, as are normal wear and tear, instances of abuse, and improper installation. Merillat's Classic, also a semicustom line, has a 25-year warranty.

Four Ways to Assess Quality

Experts agree on what distinguishes a quality semicustom cabinet: box construction, drawers, doors, and finish. In addition, hardware—drawer slides and door hinges—should be well-made and adjustable. Blum, Grass®, and Häfele are examples of top-quality hardware brands.

BOXES

Today's semicustom cabinet boxes can be made from plywood, particleboard, or medium-density fiberboard (MDF). Even if different boxes meet the same testing requirements and have equal warranties, there are variations to note in the materials used.

To begin with, not all plywood is created equal. There are different grades, and the number of plies can vary. Assuming high-quality glue and fabrication methods are used, the more plies a panel has, the more stable the panel will be. Plywood is typically the most expensive option for cabinet boxes.

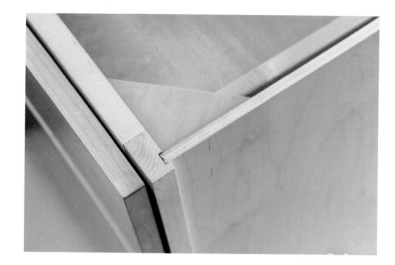

BOXES. Semicustom cabinet boxes are most often made of plywood, particleboard, or MDF.

Another option, formaldehyde-free particleboard (sometimes called furniture board), is not the cheap, porous particleboard of the past. It is a dense and durable substrate for veneer and is often more affordable than plywood cabinet boxes. It can be sized and cut with great precision, as can MDF.

MDF is made from recycled wood fibers and resin. As the smoothest of the three box materials, it is an excellent substrate for both veneer and paint. MDF's downside is its heaviness.

DRAWERS

You're likely to find dovetailed and doweled drawer construction in most semicustom cabinet lines. Both are equally sturdy, though dovetails add character and a high-quality appearance. You won't likely find glued or stapled drawers in semicustom cabinets. If you do, consider upgrading. Dovetails and dowels not only look better, but they last longer.

For a durable drawer, the hardwood or MDF fronts should be applied to a four-sided drawer box, not used as the fourth box side. Drawer boxes typically have ½-in.- or ¾-in.-thick solid-wood sides, although Canyon Creek's semicustom lines feature a ½-in.-thick plywood drawer box. A drawer bottom of 3⁄16-in.-thick plywood resists deflection

DRAWERS. Look for dovetailed or doweled drawers, which are sturdier than drawers that are glued or stapled.

DOORS. Doors aren't as clear an indicator of quality as boxes or drawers, but they should be high quality with good hardware.

even when fully loaded. Some semicustom European lines offer metal drawer boxes; a different look, it's perhaps the most durable option available.

When it comes to drawer hardware, full-extension slides separate semicustom cabinets from most stock offerings and provide full access to the contents of a drawer. Undermount slides support the drawer from the bottom; their concealment is aesthetically preferable to side-mounted slides, particularly with dovetailed drawers. A soft-close feature, available on many semicustom cabinets, means they'll close quietly and without slam damage. Avoid drawers that shake or rattle when you operate them, which is a sign of cheap drawer slides.

DOORS

Doors don't express a cabinet's overall quality as reliably as the other three items. Even lesser-quality cabinets may have reasonably well-built doors. In any event, look for ¾-in.-thick doors made of hardwood, painted or veneered MDF, or veneered particleboard. Good particleboard is dense (Merillat

Classic doors call for 48-lb. particleboard). All doors should have rubber bumpers to cushion their closing action and adjustable hinges from a reputable manufacturer.

Most doors consist of a four-piece frame plus a center panel. A center panel needs room to move in response to humidity, but that doesn't mean it should rattle around in the frame. A center panel may be hardwood or veneer, but its grain and color should closely match the frame. High-quality doors have a raised center panel set into the door frame facing either outward (a raised-panel door) or inward (a recessed flat-panel door). Raised panels— whether facing in or out—possess a thickness and solidity that distinguishes them from a ¼-in.-thick, flat center panel. Because they do not respond to changes in humidity, MDF doors in a raised-panel style are made of a single piece of material.

Door-edge, frame, and raised-panel profiles can be varied to individualize a semicustom door style, though not every style will be available for both framed and frameless cabinets. There are also

laminate and thermofoil door options, but they are more commonly found in stock cabinetry.

FINISH

Finish choices vary as much as door styles. Canyon Creek, for example, offers nearly 40 standard stain and paint colors on more than 10 wood species. Glazing, distressing, burnishing, and antiquing add subtle finish variations. Canyon Creek will also mix a finish color to match a paint-store chip.

Stain finishes comprise several steps, usually including stain application, heat curing, one or more sealer coats, and a topcoat. Cabinets are sanded by machine and by hand prior to staining, then sanded again between sealer coats. Companies typically cure stains, sealers, and topcoats with convection heat. The resulting baked-on finish is durable enough to support extended warranties.

Bertch® Cabinetry uses a blend of alkyd, amino, and vinyl resins in its sealers; the topcoats are alkyd and amino resins formulated into catalyzed conversion varnish. Sheen levels can be modulated from matte to glossy by varying the topcoat formulation, but all sheens should be equally durable.

"Painted" finishes are achieved using colored (opaque) catalyzed conversion varnishes. These dry harder than standard paint. Even when a semi-custom manufacturer matches, say, a Benjamin Moore® color, the resulting paint differs from what's available in retail because the cabinetry formulation must be sprayable and yield more sheen. The paint typically is applied as a primer coat topped with one or more additional coats, with sanding and heat-

WHY SO MANY LINES? MasterBrand Cabinets alone has eight cabinet lines ranging from stock to custom. Its semicustom lines include Homecrest, Schrock, Kemper, Kitchen Craft, Diamond, and Decorá. According to Stephanie Pierce, MasterBrand's design studio manager, each brand is tailored to a slightly different customer.

FOR FUNCTION. MasterBrand's Diamond line, shown above and left, is designed and marketed toward busy homeowners who value flexibility and function.

curing in between. Not all painted finishes receive a separately formulated topcoat as stain finishes do.

A painted finish must be applied to a smooth surface, so paint-grade maple is often used. Because this finish sits on the wood surface instead of moving into the wood like a stain, a painted finish can crack when the wood under it moves. Hairline cracks appear at door and face-frame joints, and are not considered defects. However, the finish should not peel or flake. Most manufacturers offer matching paint for touch-ups along with a cabinet order.

To assess a finish, you need to see actual product samples. The finish should be clear; a cloudy appearance is a sign of poor quality. It should be smooth and drip-free, without visible sanding marks. Molding and door edges should

FOR STYLE. MasterBrand's Decorá line, shown here and above, is meant for style-savvy homeowners who want lots of options for personalizing their kitchens.

be crisp, with no finish buildup. Low- or no-VOC formulations are desirable.

We Can't Tell You What It Will Cost

It would be great to read an article or visit a website and get a firm figure for what your cabinets might cost, but it's not that simple. Calculators can give you a range, but the offerings of semicustom cabinetmakers are vast, and even some seemingly logical questions—such as whether face-frame or frameless cabinetry is more expensive—are not so easy to answer.

Let's explore that example: Frameless boxes ought to be ¾ in. thick to provide good purchase for door hardware, whereas a face-frame box can be ⅝ in., because door hardware is not attached to the box. So frameless cabinets, in general, must be more expensive. But without face frames, those European-styled cabinets don't use as much hardwood or require as much labor. So it seems that traditional cabinets must be more expensive. But filler strips can mar the clean lines of modern, frameless cabinets, so you'll want to specify custom box dimensions, increasing the cost. You still haven't specified a door and drawer style, a finish, or all the storage upgrades you want.

In short, distinguishing by frameless or traditional construction, dovetail or dowel joinery, or one particular feature or finish is not a meaningful way to compare prices. For every instance where one company's product costs more, there are others where you will find the opposite. Showrooms offering semicustom lines have a list of "retail" prices for every component in a cabinetry manufacturer's line. (Merillat's 2011 book for its Masterpiece line runs 664 pages.) What the showroom charges a customer, however, depends first on its discount calculation—a percentage assigned by the manufacturer—and then on how it adjusts that discount to cover its cost of business. The discount calculation varies based on the dollar volume of that cabinetry line sold by that showroom, among other factors.

The purchaser's price for a kitchen with dozens of components might include upcharges for customized dimensions, premium wood species, certain finishes and hardware, or glass doors (which require a finished cabinet interior). How badly a showroom wants the business can also affect price comparisons between showrooms. With so many factors influencing the final price, you'll have to talk to a designer or dealer to get a legitimate estimate.

SOURCES

There are far too many semicustom cabinet manufacturers to list. Here are a few to get you pointed in the right direction. To dig deeper, go to a local kitchen showroom or visit the Kitchen Cabinet Manufacturers Association website (www.kcma.org).

CANYON CREEK CABINET COMPANY
www.canyoncreek.com

KRAFTMAID CABINETRY
www.kraftmaid.com

MASTERBRAND CABINETS, INC.
www.masterbrand.com

MERILLAT
www.merillat.com

Best-Value Appliances

BY SEAN GROOM

Whether you're building a new kitchen or updating the appliances in your old one, you'll quickly discover a dizzying universe of proliferating product lines and models with only slight differences between them— leaving you wondering how to get the best value for your dollar.

The multitude of appliance brands and models available today is no accident. Manufacturers purposely target narrow market segments by both price and cooking interest. Each appliance brand or collection aims at a focus-group-tested and divided market, often with a backstory or character traits assigned. GE®, for instance, breaks kitchen users into four types: *aspirer* (passionate but learning), *enthusiast* (passionate with ability), *laborer* (ambivalent with ability), and *reluctant* (without enthusiasm or ability). The features bestowed on a model depend on the consumer segment it targets, overlaid with a "good-better-best" marketing strategy. For example, Bosch® has its 300, 500, and 800 series of appliances. GE has its Profile, Café, and Monogram collections, and it recently added the Artistry series.

Another strategy is for a large holding company to market different brands targeted at different types of customers. Frigidaire® and Electrolux®, for example, are the "value" and "upscale" brands of the same company. And Whirlpool® Corporation sells products under at least five different brands: Whirlpool, Maytag®, KitchenAid®, Amana®, and Jenn-Air®.

In the Whirlpool family of brands, Amana is targeted at customers whose first priority is efficiency. KitchenAid is aimed at serious cooks who can't—or won't—spring for Whirlpool's premium Jenn-Air brand. GE has targeted its Café series at aspirers and its Monogram series at enthusiasts. The difference in features is noticeable, although it's the cheaper Café models that often have more features because they're aimed at helping people learn to cook. These features make cooking fun, easy, and engaging for the neophyte. Monogram is clearly a descendent of the commercial kitchen. In the words of GE product manager Steven Hopmann, "Monogram is about refined elegance and superlative quality." Monogram appliances look and feel more robust and cost about 35% more than those in the Café line.

There's a cachet associated with a luxury brand, so appliance manufacturers tend to position their wares toward the upper end of the market. Even though its three major-model series span the kitchen-appliance category, Bosch claims

(*continued on p. 70*)

REFRIGERATION

If you make energy efficiency a priority for any appliance, it should be the fridge. That's the Department of Energy's take as well. The DOE rolled out new energy-use requirements for refrigerators and freezers, lowering maximum annual energy consumption by about 25%. In response almost every manufacturer introduced more-efficient models. (Those meeting the new standard have a black background in the center of the familiar yellow Energy Guide sticker.)

Refrigerator prices generally increase with the number of doors and the degree of integration with surrounding cabinets. A higher price also gets you more capacity and ice-and-water dispensers. Inside, however, the glass shelves and plastic trim in a mid-priced refrigerator are similar to what you'll find in a Sub-Zero® built-in that costs four times as much. What does vary is the ease of access to bins and shelf-height flexibility, but that isn't always consistent with price. Hands-on testing is the only way to see what works best.

A higher price gets you better humidity control between freezer and fridge from dual evaporators or dual compressors, which means foods will keep longer. You'll also find LED lighting and mechanical air cleaning in models priced above $2,000.

Internet connectivity has also made its way to refrigerators. Whirlpool's 6th Sense–enabled models allow you to change your refrigerator's temperature from your smartphone. LG®'s ThinQ system promises, among other things, the ability to track refrigerator inventory and expiration dates. When a future version tracks inventory after scanning receipts or product bar codes, this could save time and money. For now, though, the amount of data that needs to be entered into your smartphone makes it highly impractical and unlikely to be used.

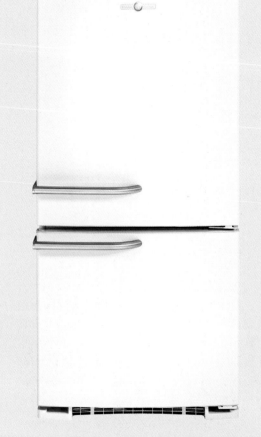

BASIC FRIDGE, BETTER DESIGN. GE's Artistry fridge is a fairly simple model with basic storage. The side-opening bottom-freezer door makes access awkward, but a high-gloss enamel finish, gently curved stainless-steel handles, and an arched door offer a unique style.

THRIFTY

Consider: Frigidaire, GE Artistry, Whirlpool
If efficiency is your primary concern, you'll save a lot of money on a refrigerator. Basic, small (16 to 20 cu. ft.), top-freezer models without features such as ice makers or water dispensers top the efficiency list. They are available for less than $700 and consume 335 to 360 kwh/yr of electricity, which costs about $40. They offer basic shelf flexibility, two crisper drawers, and at least one door shelf that holds gallon-size containers.

Bottom-freezer configurations place the most-used groceries at eye level. Prices start around $1,100 for 20-cu.-ft. fridges and approach $2,000 with an installed ice maker, stainless-steel doors, and an extra 3 cu. ft. of capacity. Side-by-side configurations are available in this price range, but they don't do well in terms of energy use or refrigeration performance.

SAVOIR FAIRE. LG's French-door refrigerator (LFC22770ST) offers great visibility and access to refrigerator items as well as a 10-year warranty on the compressor. Multiple temperature and humidity sensors and airflow channels regulate temperatures.

VALUE

Consider: GE Cafe, GE Profile, Kenmore®, KitchenAid, LG, Samsung®, Whirlpool
The first French-door models had a bottom pullout freezer and split swinging doors on the refrigerator. Newer four-door versions have a wide refrigerator drawer between the armoire-style double doors and the freezer drawer. With lots of visible sealed drawers that have adjustable humidity, French-door models are great for storing fresh food. Energy consumption is about 200 kwh/yr more than with a top-freezer model, but these fridges offer LED lighting, digital controls, a large amount of flexible storage, and filtered-water dispensers. Counter-depth models are also available in this price range, as well as various air-freshener technologies that promise to make that open box of baking soda unnecessary.

SPLIT PERSONALITY. Sub-Zero's refrigerator and freezer columns can be installed side by side, as shown here (IC-24R and IC-24FI), or in separate areas of the kitchen. Available with polished stainless-steel doors or outfitted with panels for an integrated look, they have wonderfully beefy, smooth-operating hinges and magnetic seals on all four sides of the door to ensure freshness. The interiors, however, are not that different from a less expensive fridge; there's only so much you can do with glass and plastic.

LUXURY

Consider: GE Monogram, Jenn-Air, Liebherr®, Sub-Zero, Thermador®, Viking®
Integrated and built-in refrigerators are the most expensive. These are 84-in.-tall (traditional fridges are 70 in.), large-capacity, counter-depth units that are available in a variety of door configurations, including refrigerator- and freezer-only "columns." Water dispensers, if offered, are often inside the door to accommodate panel inserts. With dual evaporators and sometimes dual compressors, temperature and humidity regulation is typically excellent, but energy performance is all over the map.

COOKING

MANY HOMEOWNERS CHOOSE the range, or the cooktop and wall oven, and then build their kitchen around this anchor appliance. Typically, the selection process starts by choosing a fuel type. For equivalent models, the price difference between gas and radiant-electric products is negligible.

Electric induction cooktops and ranges cost more than appliances run by other fuel types. A few years ago, manufacturers reserved the technology for their high-end cooktops; now there are options between $1,200 and $1,800. That's still expensive, but there's a lot to recommend the technology: It's the most energy-efficient way to cook, it boils water faster than other methods, it's programmable, and it has unparalleled heat response with precise control.

The cost of cooking appliances is driven by features and touch points. Freestanding commercial-style cooking appliances made with heavy-gauge stainless steel and sturdier doors and handles cost more. Their stylish, backlit knobs look nice, but they don't improve temperature control. Buy this type of product because it's a style statement you want for your kitchen or because you cook a lot of complex meals.

If cooking isn't a passion, you may be better served by traditional slide-in or stand-alone ranges that offer programmable controls and more timed-cooking features. You can now find ranges with induction cooktops for about $1,800. They'll bring a pot of liquid to a boil, then automatically reduce the temperature and hold it at a simmer.

CLEANING UP. LG's radiant-electric range offers two standard and two high-output elements, a warming element, and a convection oven with an infrared grill. It also boasts a 20-minute EasyClean cycle as well as a traditional self-cleaning mode for baked-on messes.

THRIFTY

Consider: Frigidaire, GE, GE Artistry, KitchenAid, LG, Maytag, Samsung, Whirlpool

You can get a basic range with a radiant cooktop or sealed gas burners and an electric oven for less than $700. Just above this price point, however, you'll start to find self-cleaning ovens, stainless-steel finishes, convection ovens, and the placement of the lower, baking element under the oven surface for easier cleaning and safety.

Doubling the price offers convenience features such as a bridge element for griddles on radiant-electric stoves as well as several oven upgrades: steam cleaning, better convection technology, fast preheat, digital controls, double ovens, and warming drawers. You can also purchase slide-in ranges with upfront controls.

SEPARATE FUNCTIONS FOR FLEXIBILITY. Whirlpool's five-burner, 36-in. gas range (GLS3665S) has all of the functions you'd expect at the $1,000 price: a high-output 15,000-Btu burner for searing and stir-frying, full-width continuous grates for sliding pots anywhere on the cooktop, and sealed burners for easier cleaning.

WORTH THE PRICE? Thermador's 48-in. Pro Grand steam range (PRD48JDSGU) is beautiful to touch, and the heavy oven doors are outfitted with dampers to prevent clunky operation. The handles fit nicely in the hand, and their solid connection to the door feels like it was welded instead of made with fasteners. Not all extravagantly expensive ranges have this solid feel.

VALUE

Consider: Bosch, GE Cafe, KitchenAid, LG, Maytag, Samsung, Whirlpool

Two possibilities in this price range offer value not available at lower price points: induction ranges and separate cooktop and wall-oven combinations. If you're motivated by energy efficiency and easy cooking, induction has a lot to offer. Separating the cooktop from the oven has the practical advantage of being easier on your back, and it offers design flexibility. Wall ovens come in single and double configurations. Double wall ovens have significantly more capacity than double ovens in a range. Among premium brands, a double wall oven and a cooktop will run between $4,000 and $4,500, but at this higher price you can gain the comfort and safety of a horizontally swinging door with Bosch's Benchmark series.

LUXURY

Consider GE Monogram, Jenn-Air, Thermador, Viking, Wolf®

Entry into the world of freestanding professional-style ranges starts at around $5,000 for a 30-in. range. Each step up in width, from 30 in. to 36 in., 48 in., or 60 in., adds significantly to cost—anywhere from $2,000 to $3,500 per increment depending on the brand. These appliances aren't wallflowers—a Viking, Wolf, Monogram, or Thermador range will be noticed for its stout presence. Other than the sheer size and number of cooking burners, the most notable feature unique to this price range is the availability of steam convection ovens.

CONSIDER A SPEED-COOK OVEN

TO MAXIMIZE VALUE AND SPACE, Jamie Gold, a San Diego, Calif.–area kitchen designer, recommends appliances that can pull double duty. She suggests clients consider a speed-cook oven instead of a second oven and a microwave. Speed-cook ovens, such as GE's Profile Advantium 30-in. wall oven (PSB9120SFSS), are smaller convection ovens that rely on combinations of microwave capability, halogen heating, and convection air movement to broil, bake, speed-cook, warm, or proof.

Some models also include a steam option. A speed-cook oven runs from $1,700 to $2,500, but it takes the place of a microwave, a second oven, and a warming drawer. By comparison, a built-in microwave typically costs $500 to $1,000, and the price differential between a single and double oven is over $1,000.

---

to target only the top 20% of the market, the idea being that its "good" models pick up where others' "best" models leave off. Brands also try to appeal to aspirational luxury: LG and KitchenAid position themselves as premium brands, as do Sub-Zero and Wolf, even though they target wildly different budgets.

GE's new Artistry series bucks this trend somewhat. The idea is simple, affordable appliances with design touches that are pleasantly retro. It will be interesting to see what hold this brand establishes in the market.

At What Price Value?

All of this raises questions of value: At what point are you paying for the reflected glory of the

brand name? Does price really indicate quality? Just how much better, for example, is a Bosch 800 series dishwasher than one from the 300 series? What exactly separates a $3,500 LG refrigerator from a $7,500 Sub-Zero? They'll both keep your food cold, right?

The good news is that, generally speaking, major brands offer quality products that work as intended. So what accounts for the variations in the scores of *Consumer Reports®'* top 40 refrigerators, which range from a high of 85 to a low of 70? Almost exclusively, it's energy consumption and ease of access to storage bins.

If efficiency is your priority, it's easy to pick out the high achievers because all fridges and dishwashers sport the Department of Energy's Energy Guide

CLEANING

DISHWASHERS ARE ALL ABOUT CONVENIENCE.
They shouldn't be heard, dishes should come out clean, and racks should be flexible enough to accommodate whatever plates, glassware, utensils, and pots you typically clean. Rated for both energy and water use, dishwashers are another place to focus on efficiency in the kitchen. Look for inline water heaters rather than exposed elements; they are a more efficient and consistent heating method. Models with turbidity sensors that evaluate the wash water for food particles can adjust cycle length as needed; fine filters with lots of surface area to trap and remove food waste reduce the amount of water used. (Filters are also quieter than motorized disposal choppers.) Stainless-steel tubs not only look better than plastic ones, but they also aid in drying the load.

If you regularly load the dishwasher with hard-to-clean items such as deep pots, baby bottles, or sports bottles, look for machines with specialty jets. Whirlpool, for instance, has models with jets mounted low on the sidewall to scrub pots; GE has models with tine-mounted jets that fit inside bottles.

THRIFTY

Consider: Frigidaire, GE, GE Artistry, LG, Maytag, Whirlpool
The first thing you'll notice about dishwashers at the lower end of the price scale is that the tubs are plastic. This savings allows manufacturers to add convenience features at relatively low cost. However, less-expensive models have less sound-deadening insulation and louder motors than more-expensive models, and likely list a 40 to 50+ dBA rating (a decibel rating for frequencies having the greatest effect on the human ear; the lower the number, the quieter the unit runs). An entry-level Maytag dishwasher (MDB6769PAS) allows the user to load the machine without having to scrape dishes, thanks to an in-unit food disposal. Maytag doesn't list the operating decibels, so it's probably relatively loud. It has a delay wash and six cycle options, including sanitize, baked-on food, and steam rinse. This Energy Star–qualified dishwasher uses 294 kwh/yr of electricity, and a standard cycle uses 4.2 gal. of water. The baked-on food cycle uses 12.3 gal.—twice that used by Bosch's heavy-duty cycles.

EMPHASIS ON CONVENIENCE. Rather than offering quiet operation and boundary-pushing energy and water efficiency, Maytag's JetClean Plus dishwasher promises "no-scrape" loading and heavy-duty scrubbing performance.

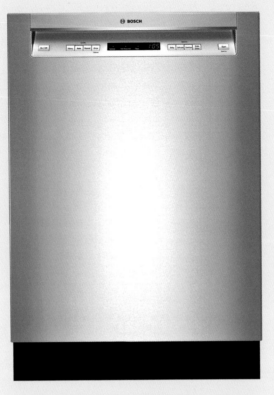

SOLID PERFORMER. Bosch's 300 series dishwashers share many features with the pricier 500 and 800 series. All three series are stingy with water consumption.

WITH A HIDDEN CONTROL PANEL and whisper-quiet operation, Bosch's 800 Plus dishwasher shines a small beam of light on the floor to let you know it's at work.

VALUE AND LUXURY

Consider: Bosch, Jenn-Air, KitchenAid, LG, Miele®, Samsung, Thermador

The shared wisdom of people I spoke with is that Bosch is a good choice if you're looking for value in a dishwasher—and that extends from the mid-range to the highest-priced models. Architect Russ Hamlet tells his clients to choose any dishwasher they want, as long as it's a Bosch. At my local independent appliance store, Holloways in Simsbury, Conn., marketing manager Laurie Donahue says that Bosch dishwashers far outsell other brands.

Bosch's models run from about $500 to nearly $2,000. What does an extra $1,500 buy you? Bosch's 800 Plus series dishwasher (SHX9PT75UC) is its quietest and most expensive. It has a flexible third rack, interior lights, an adjustable-height middle rack, and progress-indicator lights that shine a small beam on the floor. What's remarkable, though, is how many of those features are carried over to the 300 series (SHE53T55UC). Both use the same amount of water (2.9 gal.), and the 300 model uses 259 kwh/yr of electricity, only 20 kwh/yr more than the 800 Plus model. Each holds 15 place settings, has a stainless-steel tub, and is equipped with a sophisticated leak-protection system. Aside from one less wash cycle and the lack of a third rack, the most noticeable difference is likely to be sound: The 300 series runs at 46 dBA and the 800 Plus series at 38 dBA, indicating better insulation levels and probably a slightly different motor.

sticker comparing relative energy consumption. Cooling performance doesn't vary much—especially within broad price bands—so choosing a fridge in your budget range comes down to convenience features.

"It used to be if you wanted a particular feature, size, or configuration of appliance, you would have to pay top dollar," says architect Russ Hamlet. "In addition to more choices, I also see better quality and, of course, better efficiency in a lot more brands. You don't have to break the bank to get good quality with the features and looks you want."

One gauge of mechanical quality—durability—is the model's warranty. Longer warranties indicate a company's confidence in the machine's internal parts. Here's where luxury brands stand out. The standard warranty in the kitchen-appliance world is one year. The relatively affordable brand LG, however, warrants its refrigerator compressors for a decade. At the upper end of the market, Liebherr, a high-end Swiss refrigerator company, covers all parts for 12 years; includes labor on the entire appliance for the first two years; and covers labor on the sealed system for five. Another luxury brand, Viking, has a three-year full warranty and longer limited warranties (10 to 12 years) on the mechanical parts of its appliances. (This may be a response to a spate of poor-quality consumer reviews in recent years. As one industry rep told me, "Google has not been Viking's friend.")

Shop Smart

Online research is great for narrowing the field of appliance choices; you can identify the most-efficient performers, view styles, sort through features, compare prices, and read customer reviews. But a digital screen is no substitute for grasping handles, opening and closing doors, and experimenting with the function of refrigerator bins, oven shelves, and dishwasher racks.

With regard to pricing, remember that manufacturers are keen to keep people in their brand family, so you'll often find hefty rebates for each additional appliance you buy. When this article was researched, GE was offering $100 back for each additional appliance purchased; Sub-Zero and Wolf were promising a $1,000 discount when buying their refrigeration and cooking appliances together; and Thermador was willing to throw in a dishwasher with the purchase of a range. Buy one of their fridges as well, and they'd give you a free range hood.

Electric Ovens: Conventional, Convection, and Microwave

BY DON BURGARD

Most cooking is done inside the house. The typical kitchen has at least a conventional and a microwave oven; some kitchens have these plus a convection oven; and still others have ovens that combine conventional with convection cooking, or convection with microwave cooking. When outfitting a new or remodeled kitchen, it's important to think about how you cook, and then to consider your options in electric ovens.

Conventional Ovens

In a conventional oven, food is cooked through radiation and conduction: A heating element on the bottom of the oven transfers thermal energy through the chamber via electromagnetic waves. This energy heats the exposed parts of the food through radiation. It also warms the container holding the food, which then transfers heat to the unexposed parts of the food through conduction. As a result, the center is the last area to be cooked. This process is good if you like food crispy on the outside and tender on the inside. However, food looks done on the outside but isn't cooked all the way through.

The main drawback of this type of oven is that it does not create uniform heating conditions throughout the chamber. In a three-rack oven, items on the bottom rack cook most quickly because they

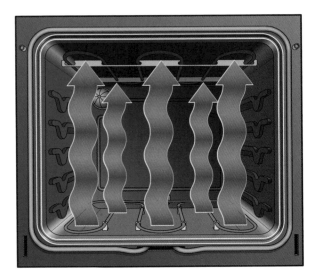

HOT AIR RISES. Set on "bake," a conventional oven produces heat from its bottom element. The top element is for broiling.

are nearest the heating element, and items on the middle rack cook the slowest. Items on the top rack cook almost as quickly as those on the bottom rack because the hot air in the chamber rises to the top.

Convection Ovens

A convection oven has heating elements on the top and bottom, and a third element connected to a fan on the back wall of the chamber. The fan moves air

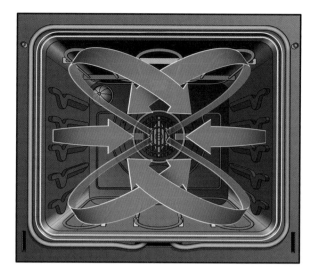

A HOT-AIR JACUZZI. In a convection oven, heat is generated by elements at the top, bottom, and rear of the chamber. A fan circulates the hot air, keeping a constant temperature throughout.

Microwave Ovens

The microwave oven has come a long way since Raytheon® introduced the Radarange in 1947. Its size, portability, and usefulness have made it a staple in kitchens, employee lunchrooms, and college dorm rooms. A microwave oven works by emitting electromagnetic waves at a certain frequency that penetrate food to a depth of up to 1½ in. These waves cause liquid-water molecules to become agitated and produce heat through friction. Areas deeper than 1½ in. are heated through conduction.

Because ice molecules, unlike liquid-water molecules, can't rotate, don't defrost on anything other than the defrost setting. The moment liquid water is present in a certain area, the microwave will start cooking that area. You'll end up with food that's cooked in some areas but still frozen in others.

in the chamber, which cooks the food more evenly than in a conventional oven. This can be observed when baking three sheets of cookies. Unlike in a conventional oven, which requires rotating the sheets through the racks for even baking, all three layers in a convection oven bake at the same rate.

Because moving air cooks more quickly than still air, the temperature in a convection oven doesn't have to be as high. A ballpark figure is to reduce the temperature by 25°F. The food will still cook faster, though; how much faster requires experimenting. Manufacturer guidelines can help here, too.

If a convection oven cooks more evenly and more quickly than a conventional oven, why haven't convection ovens replaced conventional ovens? The food in a convection oven is cooked by circulating air, so anything that impedes the air from circulating freely—such as too many dishes or pans, dishes or pans with high sides, or covered dishes—reduces the oven's efficiency. If thin-crust pizza is on the menu, therefore, a convection oven can have it ready sooner; if you're serving up a casserole, however, you're better off using a conventional oven.

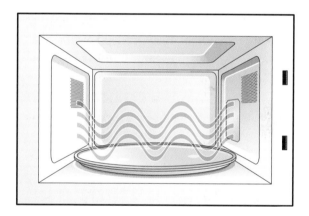

MAKE WAVES, NOT HEAT. Electromagnetic waves enter the chamber through the waveguide. A mica cover keeps food and liquid out of the waveguide while still allowing the waves to pass through.

A microwave produces waves and not actual heat, which is why you can touch the inside of the chamber immediately after cooking and not burn your hand. The microwave's settings control the percentage of the cooking time the unit is actually producing waves, not the temperature, as with a conventional or convection oven. For example, a 1000w microwave oven set at level 5 (or 50%) produces 1000w of power, but it cycles on and off at equal intervals.

Drinking-Water Filtration Systems

BY DON BURGARD

Two atoms of hydrogen and one atom of oxygen—this simple formula makes possible the presence of life on our planet. Not only do we humans owe our existence to H_2O, but we must consume it every day for optimal health. The water that comes into our homes from wells and municipal distribution systems contains more than just hydrogen and oxygen, however.

The EPA regulates 86 different water contaminants, and its most recent Contaminant Candidate List (from 2009) includes 116 additional contaminants known to exist in drinking water in the United States that the agency is considering regulating in the future.

To determine if you need to filter your water, start by obtaining your utility's consumer confidence report (CCR). Water utilities are required by law to provide this annual report, which documents the contaminants present in that utility's water system. This will give you an idea of which contaminants you need to focus on. Because a CCR applies to the system as a whole and not to your home's water supply, a more accurate picture of the contaminants you are ingesting can come only through a test of your household water. (For households whose water is supplied by a well, of course, a test is the only

A CARAFE SYSTEM such as the Brita® Capri (available at www.bedbathandbeyond.com) shown here is the easiest way to filter water.

way to find out about contaminants.) To find an approved laboratory, go to epa.gov/safewater/labs.

Carafe Systems

The easiest way of accessing filtered water is by using a carafe with a built-in carbon filter, which traps contaminants in the porous surface of its tiny granules of carbon. Many people choose these systems primarily for the way they improve the taste of tap water, mostly through reducing chlorine, which is added to public water supplies as a disinfectant. Depending on the particular system, they can reduce the presence of a number of contaminants as well. With this type of system, as with all water-filtration systems, read the manufacturer's list of contaminants the system has been tested to filter out to make sure that it includes those present in your water.

Large families may find carafe systems inadequate. The amount of water that a carafe holds may not be enough, and the short life of the filters, which last for about 40 gal. each, may require frequent changing.

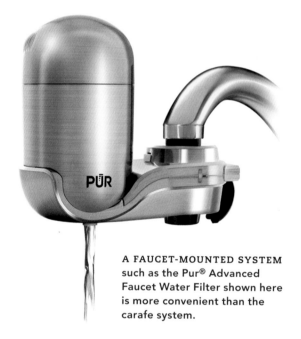

A FAUCET-MOUNTED SYSTEM such as the Pur® Advanced Faucet Water Filter shown here is more convenient than the carafe system.

Faucet-Mounted Systems

The base in these systems attaches directly to the faucet after the aerator has been removed, then a replaceable carbon-filter cartridge is inserted into the base. Though much more convenient than carafe systems, even the slimmest faucet-mounted system can look like an ugly appendage, especially if it doesn't match the finish of the faucet. (Some manufacturers offer systems in a variety of finishes.)

Depending on the model, filters in faucet-mounted systems last for between 100 gal. and 200 gal. These systems are meant to be used with cold water only; hot water can damage the filter.

Faucet-mounted systems can reduce the water flow, sometimes significantly. This optimizes the work of the filter, but it may be a nuisance if you need lots of filtered water at a given time. A switch allows you to bypass the filter when washing dishes or hands. On this setting, the flow rate is normal.

Undersink Systems

Installed (where else?) under the sink, these systems are connected to the cold-water line. Aside from the dedicated faucet they require—which allows you to run unfiltered water from the main faucet, thereby extending the life of the filter(s)—their presence is invisible. Undersink systems are available with one, two, or three filters. One-stage systems include a carbon filter. Two-stage systems may include two carbon filters, or they may include one carbon filter and one sediment filter. (If your tap water contains a lot of sediment, a sediment filter can keep the

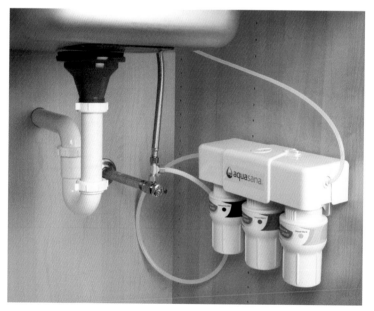

UNDERSINK SYSTEMS such as the Aquasana® three-stage system are convenient and undetectable.

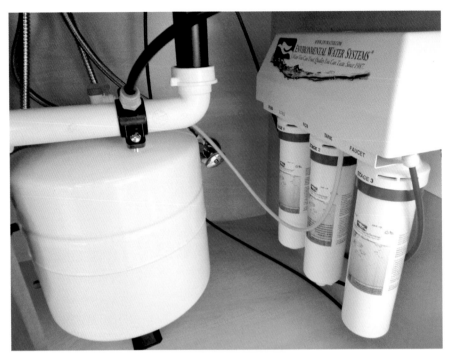

REVERSE-OSMOSIS systems such as the Environmental Water Systems® Essential RO three-stage system will thoroughly filter your water.

carbon filter from clogging.) Three-stage systems usually include two carbon filters and one sediment filter. The more filters you have, the longer you can go between changes. For example, Aquasana's three-stage system filters 600 gal., while its two-stage system filters 500 gal. and its one-stage system filters just 200 gal.

Reverse-Osmosis Systems

Reverse osmosis (RO) is a technique used by some municipalities and military units to transform seawater or water that's otherwise unfit for human consumption into potable water. On a much smaller scale, RO systems can filter household water as well.

Typically installed under the sink, an RO system begins with either two carbon filters or a sediment filter and a carbon filter. From there, water moves through a filter with a semipermeable membrane that allows water to pass but not contaminants that are larger than a water molecule. The water then proceeds to a storage tank. When the dedicated faucet is turned on, water flows directly to it or

through one more carbon filter first. The filters in an RO system usually need to be replaced annually.

RO systems get high marks for thorough filtering, but they come with at least three drawbacks. First, the large space they require limits the storage capability of the undersink area. Second, they filter out the minerals that give water its taste and that are necessary for optimal health. People who eat a well-balanced diet get most of these minerals from their food, but a study reported by the World Health Organization found that when food was cooked in demineralized water, it lost much of its mineral content. Third, the contaminants that the membrane filter traps need to be flushed out by water flowing in the opposite direction of the purified water. This water simply goes into the drainpipe. As a result, an RO system consumes far more water than it produces for drinking. In fact, a three-to-one ratio is not uncommon.

Solid-Wood Flooring

BY ANATOLE BURKIN

Solid-wood flooring has enjoyed a reputation for durability and beauty for centuries. Many older homes sport original flooring that's still in excellent condition after enduring generations of activity. With traffic and time, a wood floor develops a character and charm that's hard to beat, making it a perennially popular choice.

Whether the flooring is new or reclaimed, domestic or imported, wood offers an almost unlimited variety of finishes and can be sanded and refinished several times over its life span. The finish can simply draw out the natural character of the wood, or in the case of dye, stain, or pickling, it can color the wood. Depending on how it was cut, it can range from mild to wild in appearance. The surface can be sanded smooth (no "crumb catchers" in the kitchen), or it can be left with or given a rustic and textured look. In residential construction, solid-wood flooring is used extensively, especially in higher-end homes, because of its many creative installation possibilities, its long life span, and its purity.

In the April/May 2015 issue of *Hardwood Floors* (the magazine of the National Wood Flooring Association; NWFA), contractors reported that red oak had 43% of the U.S. market, followed by white oak at 26%. According to the NWFA, traditional 2¼-in. red-oak strip flooring is still the favorite, but there's been a trend toward wider and longer planks and toward random-width installations (a mix of 3-in., 4-in., and 5-in. planks). Also, gray colors are currently popular, as are highly figured woods containing mineral streaks, prominent grain, and knot holes.

More imported species are coming to market as well, most of them tropical woods. Flooring companies sometimes like to give them common names, but American cherry has about as much in common with Brazilian cherry as an old fashioned does to a caipirinha. Both are fine choices but wholly different flavors.

Properties and Parameters

In the marketing of flooring products, you may see the phrase *solid wood* to describe materials that contain real wood layered onto processed substrates; that product is known as engineered flooring. Solid-wood flooring as discussed here consists of 100% real wood with no substrates.

Solid-wood flooring for residential construction is typically ¾ in. thick, with tongue-and-groove joints along the edges. It can be refinished (sanded and coated) four or more times before needing replacement. The sanding process removes approximately ¹⁄₁₆ in. of material. Because the solid-wood layer is thinner on most engineered products, it is likely that it can be refinished only once or twice.

Brett Miller, vice president of education and certification at the NWFA, explains how a solid-wood floor can last for such a long time: "Aesthetically, the thickness of a floor makes no difference at all. Once it's installed, you won't be able to tell. The thickness of the wood above the tongue, however, will ultimately determine how many times the floor can be sanded and refinished during its service life. When properly maintained, wood floors can last for hundreds of years, and if repairs or sanding are required, a wood-flooring professional will remove only a small fraction of the actual flooring material. The thicker the flooring above the tongue, the more times this can happen."

Al Dobrin, sales manager and director of Amber Flooring, a custom residential and commercial flooring company in Emeryville, Calif., says that thinner material is typically used when matching a new floor to an existing floor that has been sanded down in thickness. However, the amount of material below the tongue must match the existing floor so that the replacements do not ride above the subfloor.

With solid wood, you gain the assurance that dings and scratches will still look natural and add character, in contrast to an engineered product that, if damaged to the core, will have a different color and texture than its surface.

Wood Grain and Movement

Even after wood has been cut and dried, the material will swell and shrink with changes in temperature and humidity. That's because the cells of wood are like sponges, absorbing and releasing water vapor, depending on atmospheric conditions. Floor finishes have only some vapor-retarding capability, and of course, the flooring's underside is unfinished. Floors expand and contract along their width; longitudinal movement is minimal.

In the book *Wood Flooring: A Complete Guide to Layout, Installation, and Finishing* by Charles Peterson with Andy Engel (The Taunton Press, 2010), the authors note the following: "Moisture can cause a wood floor to expand to such an extent that it actually moves the walls of a building. It takes over 1000 lb. per sq. in. to crush the wood cells

STUNNING VARIETY. Unlike a prefinished floor, where beveled edges disrupt the surface and gather dirt, unfinished solid-wood flooring can be sanded flat. This makes it possible for different lighting conditions to draw out a floor's dynamic characteristics, such as with this quartersawn white-oak floor.

of a red-oak board, yet many oak floors that have failed because of moisture-driven expansion have permanently crushed boards." That shouldn't turn you away from solid-wood floors. To the contrary, it illustrates how tough solid-wood flooring is.

How much a particular wood moves depends on two things: the individual species and how the material was cut at the mill. The greatest amount of wood movement occurs tangentially to the growth rings, which is how flat-sawn wood is cut. The least amount of wood movement occurs radially to the growth rings, which is how quartersawn wood is cut. How wood has been sawn also affects

KNOW THE LINGO

THE TERMS *GRAIN* AND *FIGURE* ARE OFTEN used interchangeably, but there is a difference. Figure is the more important of the two because it describes the most visible features of wood aside from color. When examining flooring, ask questions about how uniform or varied the wood's appearance will be from one board to the next. Flooring samples can appear remarkably uniform, but a larger presentation of the product has a far greater range of figure and color. It helps to know some of the basic terminology used to describe wood and flooring. Here's a quick guide.

ANNULAR RINGS RUN 30° OR LESS AND REVEAL A CATHEDRAL GRAIN PATTERN.

ANNULAR RINGS RUN 30° TO 60° AND REVEAL TIGHT GRAIN WITH MINIMAL RAY FLECK.

FLAT-SAWN WHITE OAK

RIFT-SAWN WHITE OAK

CHARACTER

The term character is sometimes used to refer to the presence of figure, grain, and defects. For example, salvaged lumber—with lots of pattern variation (figure), prominent growth rings (grain), and nail holes (defects)—may be described as having a lot of character. Depending on your taste, wood with character might look like junk or treasure.

GRAIN

Grain is the path in which wood fibers flow, the direction in which wood splits. In flooring, grain runs in the long direction of the strip or plank, which gives it strength. Grain can range from *open* (visually prominent), as with oak, to *closed* (visually subtle), as with maple.

COLOR

There are two aspects to color: the natural color of a type of wood and the stain or dye applied to it during finishing. Stains have pigment, and that pigment lodges in the pores of the wood, making for dramatic patterns. Dyes are more uniform and so tone the wood more evenly. Sometimes both are used. These are aesthetic choices, and more of them are available when working with unfinished flooring.

FIGURE

Figure describes the patterns in wood, many of which are unique to a particular species. Examples are ray fleck in quartersawn white oak, quilted patterns in maple, and ribbon shapes in mahogany. Not all woods exhibit dramatic figure, and it can vary greatly depending on how the wood is cut. Natural color variations within a wood such as hickory can produce what's called pigmented figure.

ANNULAR RINGS RUN 60° TO 90° AND REVEAL TIGHT GRAIN WITH PROMINENT RAY FLECK.

QUARTERSAWN WHITE OAK

TEXTURE

The oldest wooden floors were smoothed with hand tools, which left behind tool marks. During the Industrial Revolution, machines made smooth, flat floors easy to produce, so they became the norm. Today, texture choices include "hand-scraped" (usually done by a machine), smooth, and wire-brushed. At left is an example of hand-scraped maple.

GRADE

Wood is graded for quality with the terms *clear*, *select*, and *common*. Clear is the highest grade, and select has fewer of the defects, such as knots and sapwood, found in common wood.

FINISH

Most prefinished floors come with a top-coat that contains aluminum oxide, which toughens the finish. On-site finishing offers durable choices (see "Choosing the right finish," p. 85), but none can match a factory-applied finish. However, a prefinished floor has beveled edges where dirt and crumbs can gather.

the grain pattern and figure, important aesthetic considerations when choosing flooring.

For example, for a classic Craftsman-style floor, one might choose quartersawn white oak. Sawing white oak radially exposes a dramatic feature called ray fleck. Quartersawn (also known as vertical grain) wood moves less than flat-sawn, but that's not to say one should avoid flat-sawn wood for flooring. Flat-sawing is the most efficient way to cut a log, minimizing waste and allowing for wider boards. It also reveals pleasing cathedral patterns in the grain.

Installers should check the moisture content of wood before it's installed in accordance with the regional standards set by the USDA's Forest Products Laboratory. Flooring should be delivered a week or more ahead of time, left to acclimate, then installed with ½-in. expansion gaps along the walls. That way, the entire floor can expand and contract freely, like an elastic waistband. In new construction, where job sites can be damp from exposure to the elements, it's important that subfloors be allowed to dry and that wood flooring be installed at the very end of the job.

Installation and Finishes for Solid-Wood Floors

Despite the limited options, about 70% of consumers now prefer a factory finish, according to the NWFA. There are several reasons for this: Factory finishes are the most durable and come with long warranties, flooring installation is quicker and cheaper, and there is no waiting period while installers go through the time-consuming steps of sanding (which is also dusty) and applying several coats of finish.

For homeowners looking for something more specific, floors finished on-site present endless possibilities. Dyes and stains can be custom blended to match the room's decor or even the existing wood trim or existing floors. Additionally, stencils, decals, and other decorative details can be applied to a floor before the protective topcoat is added.

Ron Cutler, sales consultant and installation manager for The Floor Store in San Francisco,

outlines the finishing process his company follows: "For the finish, we typically stain and seal it, then apply two to three topcoats. With water-based finishes, it takes about seven days to fully cure. With oil-based finishes, it can take about a month to fully cure." However, floors can be walked on two days after a water-based finish is applied and three to four days for oil-based.

"When you sand the floor, you end up with a flush edge," Cutler continues. "And any gaps can be filled." That look is not possible with prefinished flooring, where there's a slight "rollover," or bevel edge, between planks as a result of finishing and milling. Also, with prefinished flooring you have to accept a height variance between planks that's about the thickness of a credit card.

According to the NWFA, water-based finishes are the most popular today, accounting for 51% of all finishes, followed by oil-modified (36%), conversion varnish (4%), oil (4%), and finishes such as wax making up the rest. "Matte and low sheens are the most popular," says Miller.

That said, custom finishes (see "Choosing the right finish," facing page) such as waxes can give a floor a warm, natural look unlike that produced from a factory finish. According to Dobrin, "A wax finish can be applied throughout the house, depending on traffic, and on average requires a new coat about every couple of years."

Adam Williams, marketing manager of the NWFA, says, "Durable film-forming prefinish options include moisture-cure urethanes, acid-cure urethanes, two-component waterborne urethanes, UV finishes, and aluminum oxides. Which is more durable is debatable."

A Designer's Perspective on Choosing Wood Flooring

Yana Mlynash, an interior designer from Mountain View, Calif., takes a logical approach with her clients when it comes to remodeling. "I always pick cabinets and countertops first and then move to floors," she says. "It's not that hard to eliminate the flooring

CHOOSING THE RIGHT FINISH

TADAS WOOD FLOORING of Naperville, Ill., specializes in refinishing hardwood floors. The company has tested many products over the years and has developed a guide that sheds light on the durability of different types of floor finishes.

	TYPE OF FINISH	TWO-PART WATER	SINGLE WATER	OIL-BASED	SWEDISH FINISH	MOISTURE-CURE	PENETRATING AND WAX	HARDWAX OILS
DURABILITY	**WEAR**	5	4	3.5	4.5	5	3	4
	SCRATCH	4.5	4	3.5	4.5	5	3	4
	CHEMICAL	5	5	4	5	5	2	4
OTHER FACTORS	**LOOKS**	4	4	5	5	5	5	5
	AGING	5	4	3	3	3	5	4.5
	FUMES/ODOR	5	5	3	1	0.5	3	5
	MAINTENANCE	4	4	4	4	4	3	5
	TIME	5	5	4	3.5	3.5	3	5
	Totals	37.5	35	30	30.5	31	27	36.5

The numbers represent the opinions of the testers and are averages for the product categories. Specific products may perform better or worse.
5 Excellent   **4** Very good   **3** Good   **2** Fair   **1** Poor   **0** Horrible

WHAT'S HOT UNDER YOUR HEELS

IN THE UNITED STATES, DOMESTIC SPECIES are by far the most commonly chosen woods for flooring. The oaks still rule, followed by maple. Among imported species, Brazilian cherry is the most popular. Below is a list of woods that details their popularity and where they are situated on the Janka hardness scale, which measures the force required to drive a 0.444-in. steel ball into the wood until half its diameter is embedded.

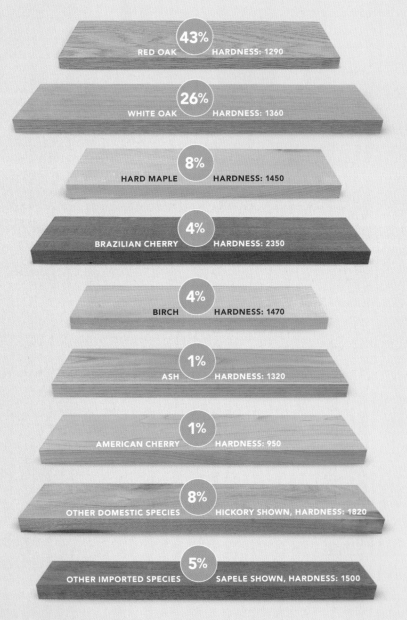

43% RED OAK — HARDNESS: 1290

26% WHITE OAK — HARDNESS: 1360

8% HARD MAPLE — HARDNESS: 1450

4% BRAZILIAN CHERRY — HARDNESS: 2350

4% BIRCH — HARDNESS: 1470

1% ASH — HARDNESS: 1320

1% AMERICAN CHERRY — HARDNESS: 950

8% OTHER DOMESTIC SPECIES — HICKORY SHOWN, HARDNESS: 1820

5% OTHER IMPORTED SPECIES — SAPELE SHOWN, HARDNESS: 1500

Source: Survey of flooring contractors as reported in the April/May 2015 issue of *Hardwood Floors*, the magazine of the National Wood Flooring Association.

options since many times it's about price, what is already in the house, and what is best for the family's situation."

But there's more to consider than simply the final product. Some families need a highly durable material (see "What's hot under your heels," left) for children and pets. Mlynash says, "You want to look at the hardness level of the floor." Oak and hickory do an excellent job of hiding scrapes and dents, especially when the flooring is salvaged.

In a remodel, choices may be limited if you prefer continuity throughout the house. "Many homes, at least in Northern California, have oak flooring," Mlynash says. "In order to not rip out the entire house, many clients choose to match the floor and sand and finish the entire house. This removes all the spotting from furniture or carpets and gives you the option of going lighter with a new stain," she said.

Unlike carpet, which can be difficult to keep totally free of mold, mildew, and dust mites, wood flooring comes clean with less effort. "Wood floors are very good for your health," says Mlynash. "They are softer than tile and easier to clean than carpet."

Shopping for flooring is a bit like buying clothes for an outfit: You need to think about how it ties together and maintain age-appropriateness. In terms of a house, that means choosing a floor durable enough to meet the tastes and tests of time, which is why solid-wood flooring is here to stay.

Resilient Flooring: Linoleum vs. Vinyl

BY MATT HIGGINS

Flooring options abound—even the options have options. But if you're looking for inexpensive flooring, especially in a potentially wet area such as a kitchen or bathroom, you're probably going to consider linoleum and vinyl. Although the terms are often used interchangeably, these materials are not the same. The mention of either sometimes conjures up images of second-rate products, but both have their place.

Linoleum and vinyl fall into the category of resilient flooring. According to Michele Zelman of Armstrong®, which makes flooring products out of both materials, to call a flooring material resilient means that it can restore its shape. If a heavy object were to land on it, the material wouldn't necessarily be permanently dented. Linoleum is mostly, but not exclusively, limited to commercial applications. Vinyl is found in numerous residential and commercial applications. Both materials are available in sheets and in tiles.

Linoleum

First patented over 150 years ago, linoleum is an older product than most people realize, and like many innovations, it was discovered by accident. English inventor Frederick Walton observed how

THE GREEN CHOICE. Linoleum is made of all-natural materials and is biodegradable, making it an affordable green flooring option.

a solid but flexible film formed on top of linseed-oil-based paint. He experimented with this natural product and eventually found it to be a perfect floor and wall covering. Since linseed oil was the primary component, Walton called his new product linoleum.

Another important characteristic of linoleum that is largely unknown—but far more relevant to current home-building trends—is that it's all natural and biodegradable. In addition to linseed oil, linoleum includes pine rosin, limestone, cork flour, wood flour, jute as the backing, and coloring pigments. Its color goes through to the backing, so scratches don't readily show. Homeowners increasingly are selecting it as a green material that is relatively inexpensive.

Linoleum must be installed over a clean, smooth, and level surface, as imperfections in the floor can cause bumps. If the surface can't be smoothed, an underlayment may be needed. Linoleum is cut with a utility knife or a heavy-duty curved linoleum knife. Typically, it's secured with flooring adhesive, and depending on manufacturer specifications, a 100-lb. roller may be used to promote strong adhesion. Seams on some products can be heat welded. Rigid click-together tongue-and-groove tiles are also available that install over a thin foam underlayment without any adhesive or fasteners. These tiles typically are cut with a jigsaw.

Linoleum isn't as flexible as vinyl, and it is more difficult to cut. There are also fewer color options with linoleum, and the material isn't used nearly as widely as vinyl. New linoleum also has a temporary yellow cast called bloom that eventually disappears when exposed to light.

Linoleum requires only basic routine care, such as sweeping and mopping with a product-specific pH-neutral cleaner, but the flooring must be polished with a sealer once or twice a year because the surface is porous.

DEEP COLOR. Because the color goes through to the backing, scratches don't readily show on linoleum.

CAN SAVE YOU SOME GREEN. Easy to install, available in an endless number of colors and patterns, and affordable, vinyl might be the right choice for your kitchen.

Vinyl

Vinyl was also discovered accidently. Waldo Semon created it in the late 1920s while attempting to develop a glue for bonding rubber to metal. Today, vinyl is, of course, used in a huge variety of applications.

Even though they are often confused and can look similar once installed, vinyl and linoleum are significantly different in terms of composition. While linoleum is all natural, vinyl is a synthetic product made using a variety of toxic chemicals, primarily polyvinyl chloride (PVC) resin. Sheet vinyl flooring also contains plasticizers for flexibility. Vinyl's large market share comes with a huge number of color and pattern options. Also, not all vinyl flooring is inexpensive. Luxury vinyl flooring (LVF, or LVT for tiles) is a higher-quality version of the product.

Like linoleum, vinyl flooring is available in sheets and tiles that get installed with flooring adhesive. A 100-lb. roller is often used, and the seams on some products can be heat welded. There is also a large selection of self-adhesive peel-and-stick tiles. Vinyl flooring is cut with a knife or shears, and since it generally is thinner and more flexible than linoleum, it's easier to cut.

PRINTED SURFACE. Vinyl's surface is inexpensive to produce and allows for great variety, but scratches can show.

Vinyl's color and patterns are printed, which allows for a tremendous variety and keeps costs low. It also means that deep scratches may show, since the color and patterns don't always go through to the backing.

Vinyl flooring requires no special care. In most cases, a mild cleaner is recommended by the manufacturer.

PART 3

Kitchen Projects

Refinish Your Cabinets

BY PHILIP HANSELL

Refinishing kitchen cabinets is a difficult and labor-intensive painting project, but the payoff can be huge. For a fraction of the cost of new cabinets, refinishing can transform a well-worn kitchen into one that looks and feels new.

As with most painting projects, the secret to a high-quality finish on kitchen cabinets is proper preparation and the right tools and materials for the job. Here, I describe how my painting company goes about refinishing cabinets in a typical kitchen. The project shown is a high-end kitchen remodel in a handsome brick house in one of the nicest neighborhoods of Durham, N.C.

The kitchen design called for new tilework, lighting, and appliances. While the built-in appliances required new cabinets, the existing cabinets were in good shape, so the homeowners decided to save thousands of dollars by refinishing their existing kitchen cabinets.

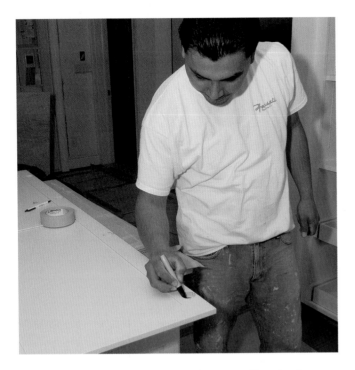

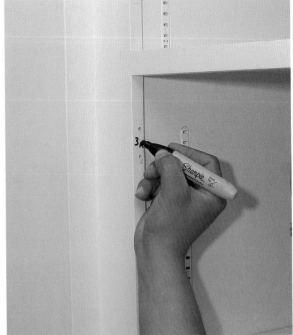

LABEL EVERYTHING. To make reinstalling the doors and drawers easier with a minimum of hinge adjustments, the crew carefully labels and bundles the hinges and marks their locations. A piece of tape covers each mark so that it won't be painted over. The marks are located so that they'll be hidden when the kitchen is put back together. Cabinet doors are marked behind a cup hinge. The mark indicates which cabinet box the door came from.

BOXES. Cabinet boxes are marked behind a hinge mount. The void in the finish will be hidden by the hinge.

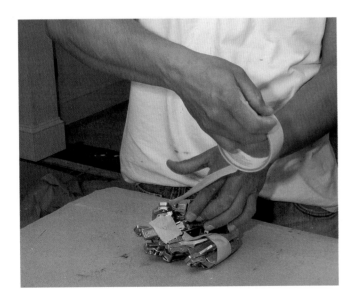

HINGES. Individually labeled hinges are grouped by cabinet door and taped together. Bundles are labeled, too.

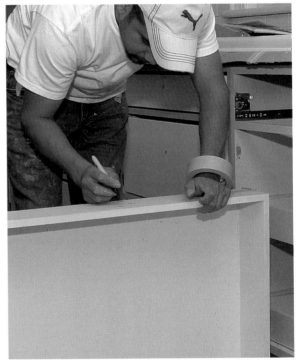

DRAWERS. Pullout shelves and drawers are labeled on the back side of the back panel to keep the marks hidden.

Spraying Works Best

Unless the client's budget is supertight, we generally paint kitchen cabinets with an airless sprayer. Spraying costs more than brushing because of the additional masking and setup, but a high-quality sprayer in the hands of an experienced painter produces a flawless, glass-smooth finish that's as good as or better than the factory finish on most mass-produced cabinets.

My company paints so many cabinets every year that we installed a spray booth in our shop. It's the same type of enclosure you'd find in an auto-body shop. Before we bought the booth, we made spray enclosures by hanging drop cloths or tarps from our shop ceiling. Tarp enclosures work fine, particularly if you'll be doing this only once, but the booth—with its bright lights and filtered air—provides a better finish in less time.

You can spray cabinets on site, too. In fact, we almost always spray cabinet boxes on the job because it's too time-consuming and expensive to remove them. Unfortunately, on most job sites it's tough to find a space large and clean enough to spray the many doors and drawers found in a typical high-end kitchen, which is why we do those in our shop.

Getting Started

The first step is protecting the countertops and floor with heavy kraft paper. If the kitchen has hardwood flooring that won't be refinished at the end of the project, we put down a thicker product called FloorShell (www.trimaco.com). We tape the paper or FloorShell® around the perimeter and at seams to prevent the high-pressure sprayer from lifting it during spraying. We also cover appliances, light fixtures, backsplashes, and adjacent walls with

SAND ALL SURFACES. Once the floor is covered with kraft paper and adjacent surfaces and hardware are masked, any damage is filled with auto-body filler, sanded with 150-grit paper, and then spot-primed with sprayed oil primer. Finally, all previously painted surfaces are sanded with 320-grit paper. Using 320-grit paper at the end creates a smooth surface for priming and painting. Changing sandpaper frequently yields quicker results.

CLEAN UP. Once everything is sanded, the kitchen is given a thorough cleaning, first with a shop vacuum and then with a damp rag. Just before spraying, cabinet surfaces are wiped with a tack cloth. All masking materials must be secured fully to prevent them from lifting during spraying.

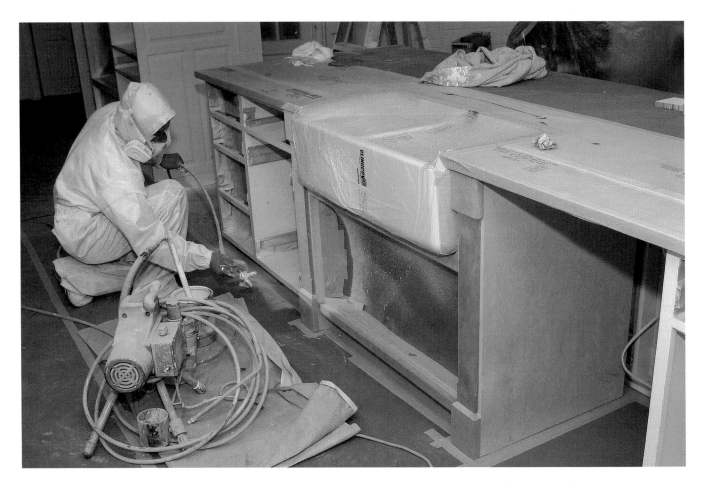

ClingCover® plastic drop cloths (www.trimaco.com) taped in place.

Refrigerators need fresh air for operation, so we leave the plastic sheeting off the intake grilles until we're ready to spray. When it's time to spray, we turn off the refrigerator and cover the grille until we're done for the day. We always tell the homeowners about this ahead of time so that they can consume or move anything that's particularly perishable.

Remove Drawers and Doors

Once the space is protected, we remove the cabinet drawers and doors. Because cabinet doors have hinges adjusted for the individual cabinet box, we carefully label the doors, hinges, and cabinets so that everything can be returned to its original location when the job is done. This saves us from having

PRIME AND PAINT. Both old and new cabinet boxes are coated first with an oil-based primer. The author and his crew start with a bank of upper cabinets, then spray the lower cabinets below. They work in the same direction for both upper and lower cabinets. Painting and priming in this order ensures that any overspray is covered with wet finish before the overspray dries. Dried overspray leaves a rough surface.

to readjust the hinges. We do the labeling in an inconspicuous spot and cover the identifying marks with tape so that they won't be obscured with paint when the part or cabinet is sprayed.

We remove pulls and knobs before stacking the doors and drawers in our trucks. With the drawers and doors removed, we mask the drawer slides and accessory hardware, but we don't mask shelf standards because they look better when they're painted to match the cabinet color.

SPRAY IN SEQUENCE.
The author prefers a Graco®.
395 or 695 sprayer with a
310 fine-finish tip, which has
a 6-in. spray pattern. Insides
are sprayed first, starting
with the top, then the sides,
bottom, and back. On the
cabinet exterior, the crew
starts with the sides and
then sprays the front. When
cabinet backs are exposed
(on islands and peninsulas),
all backs are sprayed at the
same time by working from
one end to the other, like a
typewriter.

Surface Prep

After everything in the kitchen is masked, we fix
any dents or scratches and sand the cabinet boxes
with 320-grit paper. Afterward, we dust off the
boxes with an old paintbrush and a shop vacuum
equipped with a bristle-type nozzle. After
vacuuming, we wipe everything down with a
damp rag and then a tack cloth.

Previously stained cabinets are fully sanded with
150-grit paper and then wiped down with lacquer
thinner before we spray on an oil-based primer.

Oil Works Best

We use oil products on most of our kitchen-cabinet
jobs. Oil-based paint bonds and covers better than
water-based products, and it sands more easily. In

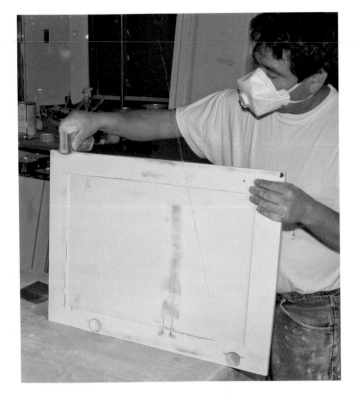

TAKE DOORS TO THE SPRAY BOOTH. Few residential construction sites have a space large and clean enough to prep and spray dozens of drawers and cabinet doors. The author takes these items to his spacious shop, where they can be prepped and then sprayed in his automotive-style spray booth. To start, gouges are filled with body filler, sanded with 150-grit paper, and spot-primed. The whole surface is sanded with 320-grit paper before painting and priming.

FRONT, BACK, BACK, FRONT. Fronts are sprayed first, followed by two coats on the back. Finally, a second coat goes on the front, minimizing handling damage to the most visible side.

addition, oil paint and primer dry more slowly than latex, so any overspray has a chance to blend in with the coating that has been sprayed on top of it. Waiting too long to cover the overspray, though, will make the surface appear rough. To minimize the rough surface caused by overspray, we spray upper cabinets first and then the lower cabinets below, and we consistently work from one end of a cabinet run to the other.

The Right Gear

For finishing the cabinets, we use a Graco 395 or 695 sprayer with a 310 fine-finish tip, which has a 6-in. spray pattern. Thinning the paint or primer is not required unless the product is especially cold, which makes the solvents more viscous. It's better to let the paint or primer warm to room temperature, however, because thinned coatings don't cover surfaces as well.

We spray primer on the inside of the cabinet box first, and then we prime the exterior. When the cabinet backs are exposed, such as on an island or a peninsula, we spray all the individual cabinet backs at the same time. Once the cabinets are fully primed and dry, we sand everything again with 320-grit paper before spraying on the topcoat.

The Right Paint

Our favorite paint for cabinets is ProClassic oil-based paint from Sherwin-Williams®. We apply it in the same order as the primer. The secret for spraying is to apply the paint in multiple thin layers to prevent drips and sags, which have to be sanded out.

It's also important that the paint be fully atomized for even coverage. If you see that the spray pattern

FINISHING TOUCHES. The last part of the job is to reinstall the door and drawer pulls. When the job calls for new hardware, the author fills the old holes, but it's the general contractor's job to drill new holes and install the new hardware. New drawer and door bumpers also are installed at this time: plastic bumpers for oil paint, felt bumpers for latex paint.

is formed by dots larger than $1/32$ in., or if there are discernible lines at the top and bottom of the spray pattern (called fingering), the paint is too thick, or you need more pressure.

Don't use a spray tip that is overly worn, and don't spray at too high a pressure. Both of these situations result in excess overspray, which wastes paint and results in a smaller spray pattern prone to drips. It's also important to hold the spray nozzle parallel to the cabinet and to start moving before pulling the trigger.

When we're done spraying, we check our work with a bright light. We make any needed touch-ups and then let the paint dry for at least 48 hours.

Reassembly

Leaving the floor and countertop protection in place, we remove the masking inside the cabinet boxes and reinstall the doors and drawers. Then we remove the rest of the masking by working from the top down so that any falling paint flakes won't stick to the freshly painted surface.

The final step is to reinstall the pulls. We also install new bumpers on the drawers and doors at this time. I like clear plastic bumpers, which are durable and soften the impact of a slamming cabinet door. Because fresh latex paint sticks to plastic bumpers, we use felt bumpers with latex paint.

Install Semicustom Cabinets

BY ISAAK MESTER

O n the face of it, installing semicustom kitchen cabinets is pretty straightforward: Attach a run of boxes to the wall, make sure all the doors and drawers work, and don't scratch the paint. Unless kitchens are a regular part of your work week, however, you'll find that the installation can go sideways in a hurry if you don't pay attention to some key aspects of the job. In demonstrating the installation of this fairly typical kitchen, I illustrate the most important tricks of the trade that help to make this a professional-looking job.

First, Unpack Carefully

The designer and the client picked semicustom cabinets from KraftMaid for the kitchen. In price and quality, they usually represent a comfortable midpoint between small-shop custom cabinets and big-box-store economy cabinets. The carcases are made of plywood, and the face frames, doors, and drawers are hardwood. The quality of the finishes is excellent. The cabinets were configured with a mix of drawer and door bases, two lazy-susan corners, and some glass-door uppers. Cabinets like these are usually shipped to the job site. The first thing I do is check the shipping manifest against the items shipped, and note any damaged or missing boxes.

The faster you start the return process, the faster you'll be able to finish the job.

When taking cabinets out of the boxes, use a knife only when necessary, and don't cut the box along the cabinet's face or you may scratch the finish. Inspect each cabinet to make sure there are no dings, and arrange the return of any damaged units.

PROTECT THE FINISH. Painter's tape on one edge of a level protects the cabinet finish. When the tape gets dirty, though, it's not helping any longer. Change it often.

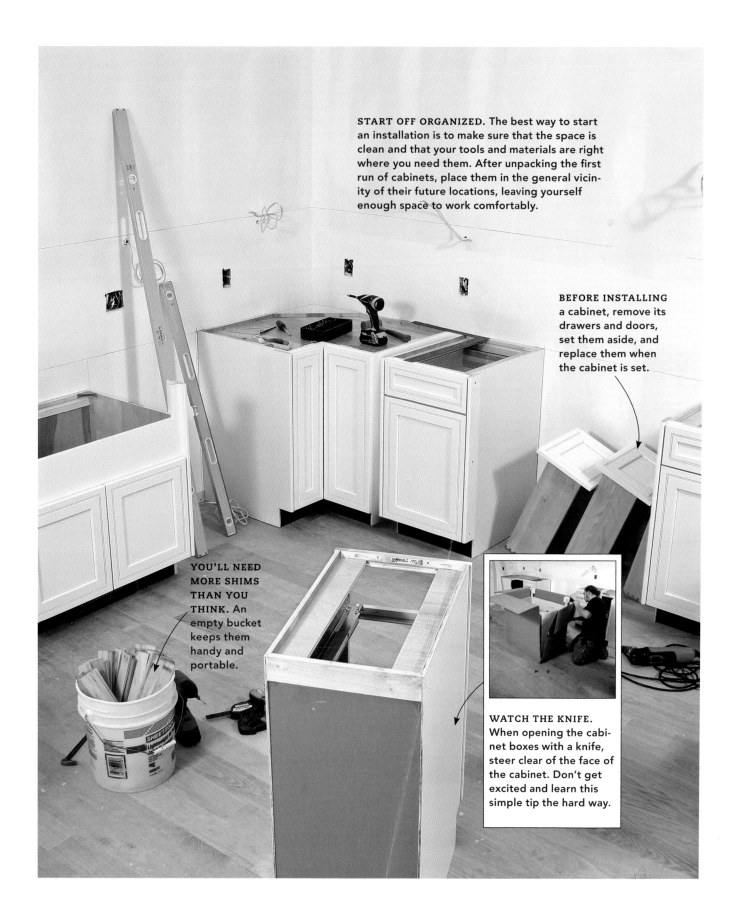

START OFF ORGANIZED. The best way to start an installation is to make sure that the space is clean and that your tools and materials are right where you need them. After unpacking the first run of cabinets, place them in the general vicinity of their future locations, leaving yourself enough space to work comfortably.

BEFORE INSTALLING a cabinet, remove its drawers and doors, set them aside, and replace them when the cabinet is set.

YOU'LL NEED MORE SHIMS THAN YOU THINK. An empty bucket keeps them handy and portable.

WATCH THE KNIFE. When opening the cabinet boxes with a knife, steer clear of the face of the cabinet. Don't get excited and learn this simple tip the hard way.

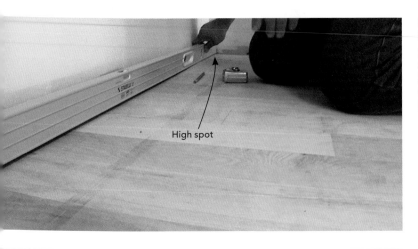

High spot

FIND THE HIGH SPOT. Use a 6-ft. level to find the highest point in the floor, which becomes the reference point to set the cabinets. Extend a level line outward to determine how much the adjacent cabinets will have to be shimmed. If the gap at the end of the run is too large to mask with trim, you'll need to adjust (see the photo at bottom left).

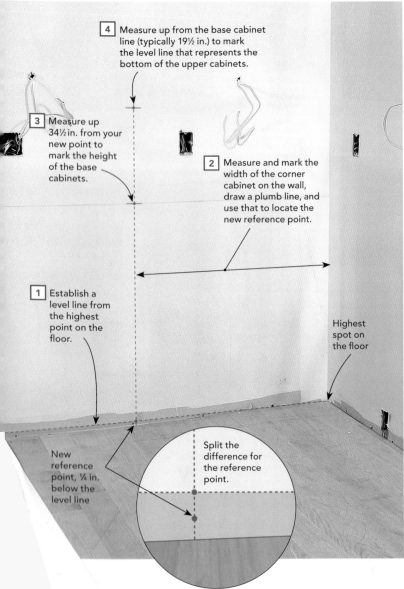

4 Measure up from the base cabinet line (typically 19½ in.) to mark the level line that represents the bottom of the upper cabinets.

3 Measure up 34½ in. from your new point to mark the height of the base cabinets.

2 Measure and mark the width of the corner cabinet on the wall, draw a plumb line, and use that to locate the new reference point.

1 Establish a level line from the highest point on the floor.

Highest spot on the floor

New reference point, ¼ in. below the level line

Split the difference for the reference point.

Factory cabinets are manufactured in part with hot-melt glue, which tends to dry in heavy drips that can get in the way of an installation. Before installing a cabinet, scrape off any of these drips.

Measure and Mark for Level

A level run of cabinets starts from a reference point taken off the high spot on the floor or, when there are soffits, the low spot on the ceiling. It's especially important for the base cabinets to be level and flat so that they can adequately support long runs of countertop.

On this job, the kitchen's cathedral ceiling meant that there were no constraints to the upper cabinets, so we based our measurements on the floor. Using a 6-ft. level, I checked the floor along the base of the wall and found a high spot in the corner. Carried out on a level line, this would translate to a gap of more than an inch at the end of the cabinet run—too high to hide with a kick plate or shoe molding.

To avoid this gap, I moved my reference point to the end of the corner cabinet, where my original level line cleared the floor by about ½ in. I then marked a new reference point ¼ in. below the original line. From this new point, I measured up 34½ in. to establish the height of the base cabinets and drew a level line there. I then made another mark 19½ in. above that line to mark the bottom of the upper cabinets, drawing that line out level as well (photo left). When installing the cabinets, I scribed and cut the bases where the floor was higher than my reference mark and shimmed the bases where the floor was lower.

START IN THE CORNER. Spend the time to get the first cabinet perfect, and it'll be much easier to install the rest.

SHIM IT. Align shims with the wall framing so that the mounting screws lock the shims into place.

GET IT RIGHT. Many installations start in the corner, so that cabinet must be plumb, level, and square. Here, I had to cut down the corner cabinet to compensate for a high spot in the kitchen's inside corner. To make an accurate cut, I scribed the side panels (1), cut them down with a jigsaw (2), and transferred those cuts to the interior base supports (3). A couple of strategically placed shims brought the cabinet into level compliance.

WHEN SHIMMING THE FRONT OF A CABINET, keep one finger on top of the face frame of the adjoining cabinet to avoid having to look to see when the two cabinets are even.

DEDICATED DRILL-DRIVERS—one for drilling pilot holes and one for driving screws—save time.

SET CABINETS CAREFULLY. As you work outward from the first cabinet, it's important to keep the successive cabinets level and in line with the walls.

TOOLS OF THE TRADE. Use a small flat bar as a lever to gain more adjustment control when shimming a cabinet. A multitool does a clean and fast job of trimming shims without disturbing or splitting them.

ESTABLISH THE REFERENCE. When marking holes in the sink base, first find the centerline of the cabinet on the wall, then measure and mark the locations of the cabinet's side and top. Use only these two points to measure the plumbing and electrical locations.

TRANSFER TO THE CABINET. From the same two points, measure and mark the centers of the plumbing stubs and the outlet.

DRILLING FOR APPEARANCES. Drill ¼-in. pilot holes on the center marks from the cabinet back, then drill from the cabinet interior with a sharp hole saw, using its pilot bit as a guide, to minimize visible tearout.

Compensating for Corners

Once you've understood the state of the floor, you have to scope out the walls. It's a rare event when a kitchen's walls are plumb and square. I checked to see that the corner itself was relatively square so that the end cabinet on either side wouldn't flare out from the wall. Corners are often less than square because of the buildup of tape and compound. Sometimes the best solution is to cut or scrape out the compound behind the cabinet to square up the corner.

I like to join the corner cabinet to the adjoining cabinets before attaching them to the wall so that I can carry the corner outward in two directions. If the corner isn't square, I can adjust the cabinet's angles so that there's an equal gap behind the end cabinets, which I usually conceal with a finished end panel. Here, because the line of cabinets was

interrupted by appliances, I had the option of adjusting the position of the cabinets independently, but I always try to keep the counter overhang as consistent as possible.

There are times when joining your upper cabinets together on the ground will make the installation much easier and straighter. This is especially true with frameless cabinets, as there is absolutely no play in the installation. Some installers like to hang the upper cabinets first because they don't have to reach up and over the base cabinets. Many kitchen designs (like this one) are driven by appliance locations, though, so it's important to establish the base location first.

When it came to installing the upper cabinets, the first thing I did was to screw a length of scrap brick molding to the wall studs along the upper level line. This serves two purposes: First, it's a third hand to

SET UPPER CABINETS WITH A LEDGER. As with the lower cabinets, the upper-cabinet installation begins in the corner and works outward. Secondary support, such as a ledger or cabinet jack, helps to stabilize a cabinet's position while stud and wiring locations are marked and pilot holes drilled.

KEEP CABINETS IN LINE. Use padded bar clamps to attach the next cabinet in line with the first, making sure to align the face frames. Always countersink a pilot hole for screws, and use decking or similar heavy-duty screws to attach cabinets to each other and washer-head screws to attach cabinets to the wall. Drywall screws are too brittle and shouldn't be used.

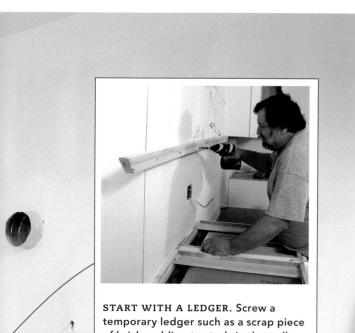

START WITH A LEDGER. Screw a temporary ledger such as a scrap piece of brick molding to studs in the wall to help support the upper cabinets. When screwing a cabinet to the wall, transfer the locations of the ledger screws to the inside of the cabinet.

MOVE THE WIRES TO WHERE THEY BELONG. Here, the under-cabinet feeds should be above the cabinet bottom. On this job, a full backsplash will conceal the drywall repair.

support the cabinets as they're installed; second, it makes a handy reference when locating screws inside the cabinet. If the area between the bases and the uppers isn't meant to be covered by a backsplash, it's easy enough to patch the screw holes in the walls.

Keep Plumbing and Electrical Neat

One of the details that adds to a good installation is careful integration of cable and pipes in the cabinets. I have encountered too many kitchens where the installers simply hacked out a square in the cabinet back for the water and waste lines, which is visible whenever the cabinet is open.

The first step I take to ensure this integration is to insist that the plumber leave everything stubbed out and capped. It makes it easier to do a careful layout, which in turn makes a neater installation.

BACKING NOT INCLUDED. Finished trim panels on the back of peninsulas often require extra nailing support. Layout lines on the walls help to locate blocking in the right places.

KEEP FASTENERS CONCEALED.
Meant to be covered by corner trim
or base, the perimeters are good
spots to attach the panels and still
keep the appearance clean.

Second, I find out what kind of undercabinet
lighting is going to be installed later so that I
can drill the holes in the proper locations of the
cabinet. There's nothing worse than seeing the lights
installed with 2 ft. of exposed wire running across
the bottom of the cabinet to the hole that I drilled.

Scribing Shouldn't Be Difficult

Once the cabinets are in, the next step is to scribe
and attach the finished end panels. Base moldings,
often part of the trim package in semicustom
cabinets, cover any gaps between the panels and the
floor, so the wall is the critical area to be scribed.
After measuring the space and determining the
correct width or length of the panel, I shim or
clamp the panel's top equal to the top of the cabinet.
Setting a compass to the distance of the largest
portion of the gap between the wall and the panel,

THE EASIEST CROWN JOB. Because of the cathedral
ceiling in this kitchen, the cabinet crown could be cut
simply by registering its spring angles onto the miter
saw's table and fence.

I scribe the wall's line onto the panel, check the measurement to make sure it's right, and cut away the waste. Full-length panels should be shimmed plumb before they're scribed.

Tips for Installing Trim

The trim for semicustom cabinets is usually made from prefinished hardwood, and it's relatively expensive and difficult to replace once you've started. Make sure you have enough before you sign off on the delivery, although distributors often can send missing pieces within a few days. Because it's prefinished, the trim must be cut carefully to avoid tearout. Keep nail holes small so they can be concealed with a color-matched filler, and glue joints for extra holding power. When working with dark-stained crown, apply stain on the inside edges of miters so that any gaps won't show as prominently.

WORK CAREFULLY WITH PREFINISHED STOCK. To reduce visible nail holes, it's a good idea to use the smallest nail or brad possible when attaching crown or other exposed trim.

Build a Clever Island with Drawers

BY JOSEPH B. LANZA

I recently renovated a carriage house that was to be used for entertaining or for extended stays from my clients' family. On the upper level, more than half of the 20-ft. by 24-ft. space was taken up by the kitchen. To make the kitchen efficient, the clients and I wanted the island to be a space for working as well as for gathering and eating.

A few issues came up as I designed the rest of the kitchen. For example, positioning the sink and the major appliances along the outside wall wouldn't leave much space for storage. To have room for seating, the island needed an overhanging counter on three sides, which left room for only two base cabinets. I knew that the big overhang would create space for drawers below the top, a detail seen on many tables. Table-style legs on an island of this size, though, would look bulky and would interfere with seating. My challenge became how to support drawers without legs. Here was my solution: Two plywood base cabinets with solid, substantial tops and backs support a frame of 5/4 poplar glued and screwed together and skinned with a piece of ½-in. birch plywood. This frame supports a countertop of solid 6/4 maple, which, in turn, stiffens and supports the frame. The frame carries the drawers on side-mount slides to save space. The base is covered with

SMART CONSTRUCTION. To get both seating and storage in this island, the top had to multitask. The key to its success is an open frame made of 5/4 poplar strong enough to support a cantilevered maple countertop, yet with space for six drawers. The addition of a layer of ½-in. plywood creates a structure stronger than the frame alone.

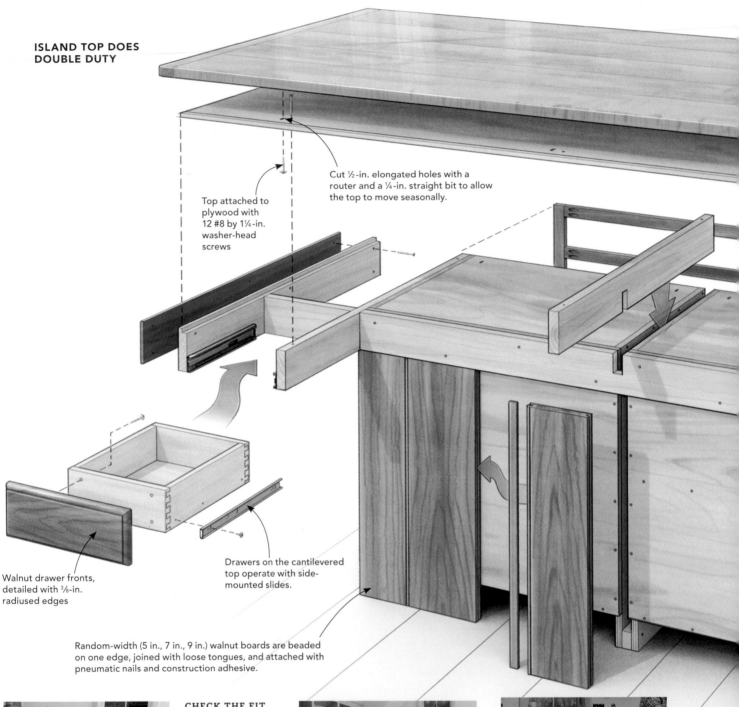

ISLAND TOP DOES DOUBLE DUTY

Cut ½-in. elongated holes with a router and a ¼-in. straight bit to allow the top to move seasonally.

Top attached to plywood with 12 #8 by 1¼-in. washer-head screws

Walnut drawer fronts, detailed with ⅜-in. radiused edges

Drawers on the cantilevered top operate with side-mounted slides.

Random-width (5 in., 7 in., 9 in.) walnut boards are beaded on one edge, joined with loose tongues, and attached with pneumatic nails and construction adhesive.

CHECK THE FIT. Because the frame's strength depends on the locations and the tightness of the bridle joints, dry-fit the entire frame around the cabinets before applying glue.

ADD THE TOP. Once the frame is assembled, measure and cut a piece of ½-in. plywood that will strengthen the base for the solid maple countertop.

EDGES CONCEALED. Although the plywood is hidden by the drawers and trim, the author recessed the plywood into the frame and covered the sides with a band of poplar.

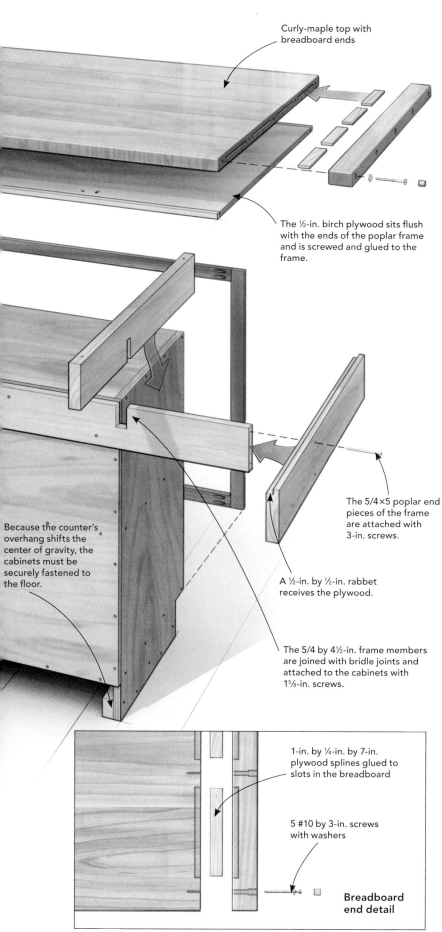

Curly-maple top with breadboard ends

The 1/2-in. birch plywood sits flush with the ends of the poplar frame and is screwed and glued to the frame.

Because the counter's overhang shifts the center of gravity, the cabinets must be securely fastened to the floor.

The 5/4×5 poplar end pieces of the frame are attached with 3-in. screws.

A 1/2-in. by 1/2-in. rabbet receives the plywood.

The 5/4 by 4 1/2-in. frame members are joined with bridle joints and attached to the cabinets with 1 5/8-in. screws.

1-in. by 1/4-in. by 7-in. plywood splines glued to slots in the breadboard

5 #10 by 3-in. screws with washers

Breadboard end detail

4/4 walnut random-width beadboard, drawers, and door fronts.

Start with the Boxes

I'm a big fan of simple cabinet boxes, and these boxes fit that category perfectly. I often use 3/4-in. birch plywood, and I glue, nail, and screw the butt joints together. I wanted these two cabinets to be able to support the big maple top, so I stiffened them with 3/4-in. backs and full (rather than strip) tops. One cabinet holds the microwave, and the other features a drawer above a pair of doors.

At the site, I marked the locations for the boxes and screwed 2× cleats to the floor just inside their footprints at each end. Between where the two cabinets would rest, I anchored another cleat the same thickness as the frame and screwed the cabinets to the cleats.

Integrate the Frame with the Boxes

To support the top and to house the drawers, I made a frame of 5/4×5 poplar that would extend beyond the cabinets approximately 14 in. To make a more positive connection with the plywood subtop, I cut a 1/2-in.-deep rabbet along the edge of both end pieces and ripped the remaining pieces down to 4 1/2 in. I cut bridle joints at the appropriate points and attached the frame with glue and screws. I cut the plywood to size, and screwed and glued it to the top of the frame.

Final Assembly

Back at the site, I installed the face frames and attached the beadboard. After installing the drawers and their Blum undermount slides on the work side, I hung the doors and the drawer fronts. On the seating side of the island, I installed the drawers with Accuride®-style side-mount slides. I completed the job by finishing both the walnut base and the maple top with three coats of Ceramithane®, a waterborne urethane.

Install
Crown Molding

BY GARY STRIEGLER

When I started building, ceilings were 8 ft. tall. In the kitchen, a clunky soffit dropped down a foot above the cabinets, limiting them to 7 ft. in height. When ceiling heights grew to 9 ft., kitchen cabinets grew another foot or so to about 8 ft. Who couldn't use the extra storage? But that was the limit for kitchen cabinets, because close to no one can reach higher than that without a ladder. Still, in my market, ceiling height continued to grow to about 10 ft. What do you do with the space above the cabinets? One solution is to leave it open as display space. Of course, that adds costs for lighting and display items, never mind the extra dusting.

In response, some of my clients asked about taking their upper cabinets all the way to the ceiling, which at least minimizes the dusting. But just growing the upper cabinets by 2 ft. would put the proportions way out of balance. Plus, manufacturers don't want to warrant a door that tall. One solution was to add a set of short cabinets with glass doors. That cuts way back on the dusting, and the extra row of cabinets looks great. However, it can add several thousand dollars to the cabinet budget. I needed a third option that would be less expensive than adding cabinets and involve less maintenance than open tops. The solution turned

TWO POINTS MAKE A LINE. Use a level to plumb up from the face of the cabinet and to establish the endpoints of the cleat.

Cleat

Crown molding

Frieze

Panel molding

Bolection
molding

Cabinet

NAIL THE CLEAT TO THE CEILING. If the cleat crosses joists, nail to them. If not, spread glue on the back of the cleat, and secure it while the glue sets by driving nails at opposing angles into the drywall.

out to be adding a decorative frieze above standard wall cabinets.

The whole assembly is relatively inexpensive to build, consisting merely of a flat frieze board that supports crown, panel, and bolection molding. It looks great, ties into the kitchen crown molding, and needs little dusting. It took my lead carpenter and me a bit over a day to build the frieze for the kitchen shown here. Kitchens vary, of course: Ceiling height, cabinet height, style, and finishes will affect your final design. Because this custom kitchen was later painted on site, the frieze ended up blending seamlessly with both the room and the cabinets. If you use prefinished cabinets, you can get finished

ADD A NAILER FOR THE CROWN

WHEN THE JOISTS RUN PERPENDICULAR to the cabinets, they provide nailing every 16 in. When they don't, a piece of 2× stock glued to the drywall offers a solid attachment for crown. Once it dries, carpenter's glue does a surprisingly good job of holding the nailer in place. The trick is securing the piece until the glue dries. For that, drive in long finish nails at opposing angles.

2× stock

REINFORCING A CORNER. When there are no joists at a corner, reinforce the cleats by adding a second layer.

MARK THE CABINET. Because the frieze board and the tops of the doors are so close, any variation in spacing between the two would be obvious. Mark the frieze location carefully.

plywood and moldings from most manufacturers that can be used in the same way.

Cleats Outline the Frieze

I fasten the top of the frieze to cleats nailed to the ceiling and plumb with the face of the cabinets. To ensure that the top of long runs of frieze will be straight, I establish two endpoints and snap a chalkline on the ceiling. I make the cleats from scraps of whatever the frieze-board material is—in this case, ¾-in. MDF. The material doesn't matter as much as making sure it's straight so that any irregularities don't telegraph to the face of the frieze.

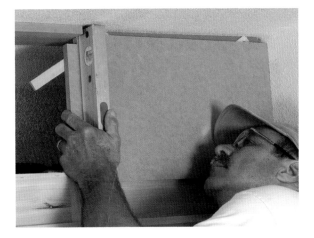

CHECK FOR PLUMB. To ensure tight joints, it's crucial that the frieze be plumb. Sometimes a shim or two is required.

Frieze Board Is the Foundation

Because this kitchen was going to be painted, my lead carpenter and I ripped the frieze board from ¾-in. MDF shelf board. MDF is stable and holds paint well, and shelf board is a convenient way to buy it. We mitered the outside corners and butted the insides. The inside and outside corners had to look good, but the fit against the ceiling and the tops

NAIL THE FRIEZE BOARD. Be sure to hit both the tops of the cabinets and the cleats on the ceiling.

NOTCH, AND ADD NAILERS AS NEEDED. Some pieces of frieze board will extend behind others. Notches allow them to clear the cabinets and the cleats. Nailers provide attachment for the abutting frieze board.

MARK THE CROWN'S BOTTOM. Use a block cut to the length of the crown's drop to mark the location of the crown's bottom on the frieze.

MARK THE CROWN'S TOP. To locate the top, hold a scrap of crown to the bottom line.

of the cabinets didn't matter much since we were adding moldings in both places.

Mark the Crown's Location

When installing crown molding for cabinets, the lengths are typically short, so I like to mark the crown for cutting by holding it in place. To ensure I'm holding it at a consistent angle, I mark the location of the crown's top on the ceiling and its bottom on the frieze board. I determine the crown's drop from the ceiling by holding a scrap inside a square and noting the measurement, which I use to make a gauge block.

Cutting Crown Miters on the Flat

Wider crown, such as the 7-in. material used here, can't be cut standing up on most miter saws, so it has to be cut lying flat. If the crown is the most common configuration, which springs off the wall at 38° and meets the ceiling at 52°, set the saw at a 33.9° bevel and a 31.6° miter. Most compound-miter saws have marks or detents at these locations. Many newer saws bevel to the left and the right, but older saws as well as some new ones bevel to one side only, usually with the saw tilting to the left, as shown on the facing page.

THE MOST COMMON CROWN CONFIGURATION

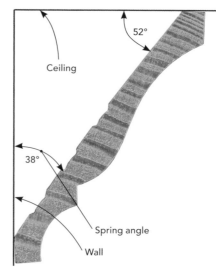

CUTTING CROWN MITERS

SET THE MITER ANGLE TO THE LEFT

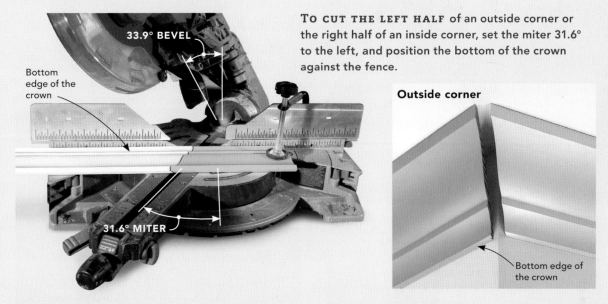

33.9° BEVEL

Bottom edge of the crown

31.6° MITER

TO CUT THE LEFT HALF of an outside corner or the right half of an inside corner, set the miter 31.6° to the left, and position the bottom of the crown against the fence.

Outside corner

Bottom edge of the crown

SET THE MITER ANGLE TO THE RIGHT

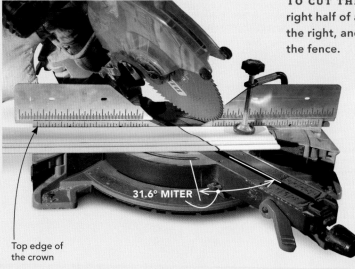

31.6° MITER

Top edge of the crown

TO CUT THE LEFT HALF of an inside corner or the right half of an outside corner, set the miter 31.6° to the right, and position the top of the crown against the fence.

Inside corner

ASSEMBLE SHORT SECTIONS. Use glue and brad nails to join short sections to longer pieces prior to installation.

NAIL IN PLACE. Holding the crown on the lines, fasten it to the frieze and ceiling.

FASTEN THE JOINT. Spread some glue inside the joint, and reinforce it with brads.

Tackle Tough Pieces First

I start with the most difficult sections, which are typically the short ones, or where there's a piece with two inside corners. Sections with short runs are easier to assemble on a bench; that way, you're sure to get a tight fit. I cut one end of the longer sections, then hold the pieces in place to check the fit before marking the other end for cutting.

ADD A SACRIFICIAL SHIM UNDER THE BOLECTION WHEN CUTTING. To get the correct angle, make the shim the same thickness as the piece the molding lips over.

NAIL THE BOLECTION HOME. Hold the lip of the bolection molding tight to the edge of the frieze when nailing.

LOCATE THE BOTTOM OF THE PANEL MOLD. Holding a block against the crown ensures a consistent line.

MARKING IN PLACE MAKES FOR ACCURATE CUTS. Make sure the first end of the piece fits well, then mark the second end with a sharp pencil.

Bolection Molding Adds Interest

I had options for the panel molding below the frieze board, but I selected a bolection molding (see the photos at right on the facing page). Most panel moldings (also known as base cap) are ¾ in. thick and would just butt up to the frieze. Bolection molding is milled so that the top edge of the molding lips over the piece above, hiding the joint as well as adding depth and interest. When being cut, bolection molding has to be held at the angle it will be installed.

Panel Molding Breaks Up a Wide Board

Adding a panel mold below the crown breaks up the wide frieze and adds interest. I find that placing the band of panel molding about two-thirds of the way between the crown and the bolection is about the right proportion. Unlike the crown and the bolection, panel molding is simply cut flat against the fence.

NAIL THE PANEL MOLDING ALONG THE LAYOUT LINES. Particularly with longer pieces, installing along the lines straightens any warped molding.

Tile a
Backsplash

BY TIM KEEFE

Kitchen backsplashes are among my most frequently requested tile jobs. Whether a backsplash is part of a new construction project, a full kitchen remodel, or a quick update of an existing kitchen, few other tile projects can bring such a huge transformation to such a contained area.

Although more-modern varieties of tile are common, the classic look of 3×6 subway tile never seems to go out of style, and I'm asked to install it often. In this particular kitchen, the homeowners decided to boost the look of their subway backsplash by choosing crackle-glazed tiles and including a section of mosaic tile above the range. This particular type of tile and the use of a mosaic accent are options that are growing in popularity, and each holds its own challenges in terms of layout and installation.

Done right, this combination of a subway-tile field and a mosaic-tile accent becomes a beautiful background for the kitchen. Done poorly, either in terms of layout or installation, the backsplash becomes a daily eyesore. The good news is that a pleasing layout isn't hard to achieve, and the process of laying up and grouting tile isn't complicated, as long as you plan carefully and work through each step slowly.

Before All Else, Set Up and Prep

When I'm installing a backsplash in a finished house, I typically don't set up the wet saw inside. Putting the saw outside or in the garage eliminates the risk of water damage to the floor. I cover the countertops and the floor—EconoRunner (www. protectiveproducts.com) is an excellent choice—and if the kitchen has a freestanding or slide-in range, I pull it away from the wall and cover it with a drop cloth so that I can tile behind it. After cutting the power to any electrical boxes in the backsplash area, I loosen the screws on the fixtures and pull them out of their boxes slightly so that the tile can fit tightly around them. If tile is to go around a window, I

remove the apron molding below the stool. That means less-complicated cuts, and the finished look is cleaner.

The next step, and one that far too many installers brazenly skip, is to get to know the tile. Tiles and their recommended installation practices vary widely from brand to brand and from tile to tile. If the tile comes with instructions, it's important to read them. They might mean the difference between an easy job and a nightmare installation.

The maker of the field and mosaic tile installed on this job, Encore Ceramics, recommends that these tiles be coated with sealer before installation to prevent thinset from getting trapped in the hairline

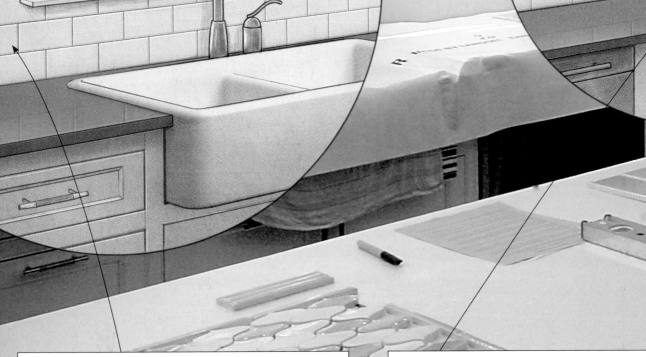

PRIORITIES FOR A PERFECT LAYOUT

ENDPOINTS

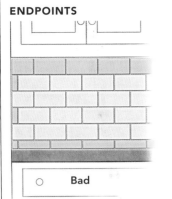

○ Bad

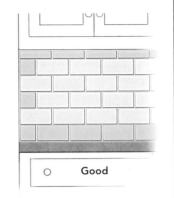

○ Good

Don't cut the first row of tile in an effort to end with a full-height row at the top. The bottom row is far more visible and should always be full-height. If a layout leaves you with awkward, narrow cuts at one end of a run, adjust the grout spacing over several feet of the wall to alter the endpoint and to ensure a half-whole pattern.

INSIDE CORNERS

Corners are a focal point. Save the mirror-image look for diagonal tile layouts. For a traditional running-bond layout, inside corners look best when the pattern flows from wall to wall, a so-called folded corner.

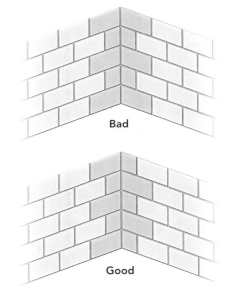

Bad

Good

MOSAIC ACCENT AREAS

Narrow cuts are OK sometimes, but not when they create a vertical grout joint in a tight space. Adjust the layout to avoid slivers of tile.

Size the accent so that the edges of the mosaic are a combination of whole and half tiles, never less or more.

Bad

Good

Tiles should line up at the top of an accent. You can sometimes cheat to make this happen by cutting custom-height tiles from the long dimension of a standard piece, and then easing the cut edge with 80-grit sandpaper to create a factorylike edge.

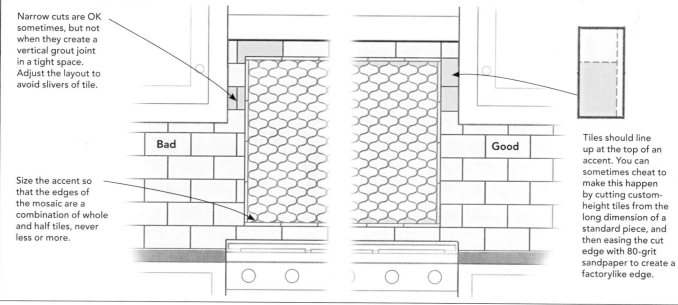

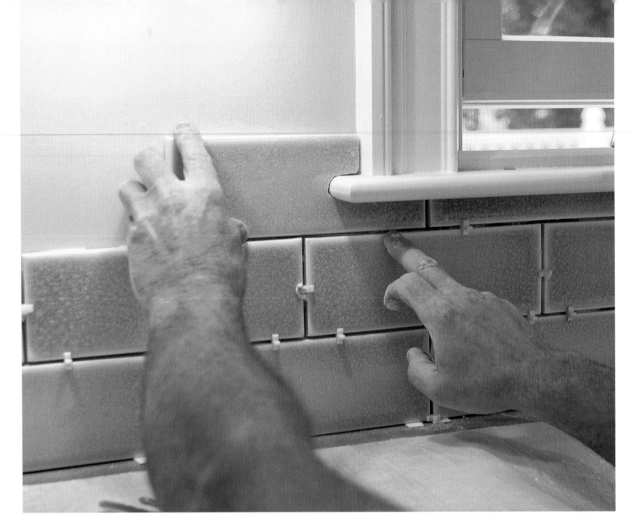

STOOLS SHOULD STAND ALONE. Scribe tile to fit around windows and stools using a diamond blade in an angle grinder to create the curves. Because it's harder to notch around the subtle ins and outs of the apron molding below most stools, remove the apron molding so that the tile can run uninterrupted below the window.

cracks of the glazed finish. It also makes it easier to remove dried globs of thinset from the face of the tiles after installation. I've had great success with products from Miracle Sealants Company.

Not Rules, but Priorities

No two backsplashes will be the same. Aside from the fact that tiles vary widely in size and shape, you also have to consider the height of the backsplash, the placement of electrical outlets, whether there is a window or not, and how the tile will terminate at the ends of a run. There are always trade-offs, which is why I approach each job with a list of priorities and work from there.

For a subway-tile backsplash like this one, my first priority is to maintain the running-bond pattern. I also always begin with a full tile at the countertop (and let the uppermost row of tiles fall as it will). From there, the layout is a bit more trial and error.

KEEP IT TIGHT AT THE OUTLETS. Cut tile so close to electrical fixtures that you have to notch for receptacle screws with an angle grinder, which eliminates the need for spacers or box extenders. This also helps avoid any concern about the coverplate not hiding your cuts.

I plan horizontal and vertical layouts around focal points, such as a range hood, an inside corner, or any other highly visible area. If the kitchen layout includes inside corners, I prefer to carry the layout from one wall to the other without deviating from the running-bond pattern. The most important thing is to do your best to avoid narrow slivers of tile butting up against cabinetry or trim. Nevertheless, they may be unavoidable in certain situations.

Finally, for mosaic tiles, such as in the accent area above the range in this kitchen, it's more about symmetry than anything else. Don't let the size of the accent area be dictated by the space; consider also the size of the tile itself. I prefer the accent area to be centered over the range, with a combination of half or whole tiles at the edges, surrounded by pencil tiles and an even border of field tile.

Install One Tile at a Time

There are two common choices for adhering tile to a wall: mastic, which is a latex-based adhesive that comes ready to use out of the bucket; or thinset,

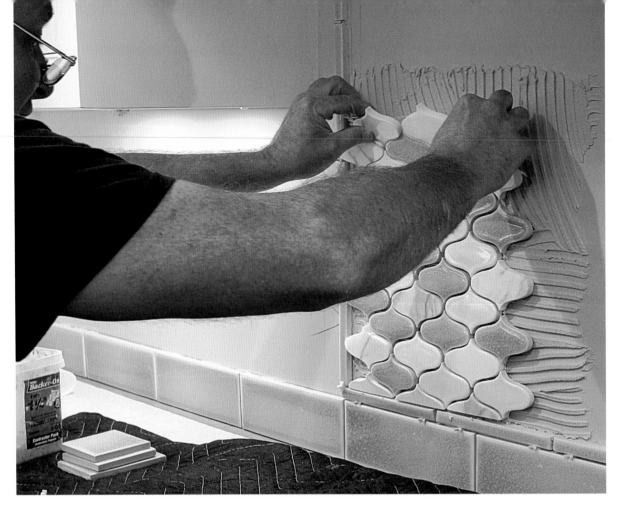

FOR ACCENTS, SYMMETRY TRUMPS SIZE. Transfer the rough dimensions of the accent to cardboard, and then modify the layout until there are even cuts on all sides. After cutting, dry the tiles quickly because some mosaic-tile sheets are held together with water-soluble adhesives.

which is a cement-based mixture that is combined with water. I don't like mastic because it shrinks as it dries, making it harder to build up any low spots in the wall. My go-to thinset lately has been Laticrete® Sure Set, a polymer-modified thinset that bonds tenaciously.

Rather than combing thinset onto the wall and throwing up tiles rapid-fire style down the line, I work more slowly. I spread thinset onto one tile, apply it to the wall, and then support and position it with spacers. Other installers might call me crazy, but I don't have to lean over the counter awkwardly while spreading thinset on the wall, I don't have to worry about the thinset skinning over if I don't work fast enough, and I have no doubts about getting good contact between cement and tile.

For the best results, thinset should be wet enough that the cement penetrates the back of the tile, but not so wet that it sags or drips off. The size of the trowel used to apply the tile also matters, even when applying one tile at a time, and it varies based on the type and size of tile being installed. For 3×6 subway tile like this, a ¼-in. by ¼-in. square-notch trowel is my preferred tool.

Grout Ties It All Together

The job of grout is largely aesthetic—it fills the gaps between tiles and smooths differences in flatness or projection from the surface of one tile to the next— but it also adds a bit of strength. I prefer Laticrete's PermaColor grout because it cures to make an uncommonly strong joint compared to other cementitious grouts. Plus, unlike standard unsanded grout, PermaColor can be used in joints as narrow as 1/16 in. wide. This grout dries a bit faster, so it has to be mixed in small batches until you become accustomed to the working time. However, it still needs to dry for 48 hours prior to sealing.

The mosaic accent area on this job was going to be grouted in a different color from the field tile surrounding it, which is not an uncommon situation. In cases like this, I start with the field tile, not worrying about any grout that oozes into the area of the mosaic accent. Once the grout firms up somewhat, it's easy to clean out the joints with

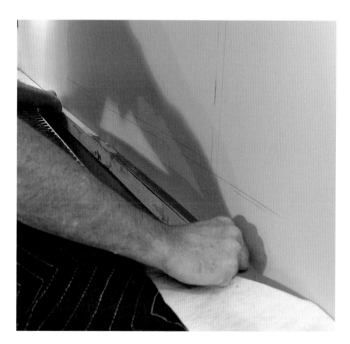

AVOID THE SCREWS. You don't need to screw in a ledger behind the oven to support the first row of tile. Instead, cut a piece of wood so it can be pressure-fit between the countertops.

GET THE MIX RIGHT. Thinset should be a creamy, peanut-buttery, plasterlike consistency. Dip a finger in the mix. If it hangs without dripping, you got it right.

STOP THE SLIDE. Screws driven into drywall offer enough holding power to temporarily support tiles that are sliding out of alignment.

a utility knife. Then when I'm ready to grout the mosaic section, the surrounding field-tile grout will have firmed up enough so that I can wipe away any overgrouting with a sponge.

The last step in the process is to apply caulk to any areas where the tile meets a hard edge. These areas include trimwork, cabinetry, a range hood, and the countertop. Most brands of grout offer a color-matched caulk for these spots, but once again, I find that Laticrete caulks are the best products available for color match.

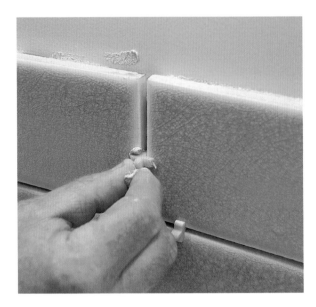

KEEP SPACERS IN PLACE. To ensure that tile spacers don't fall out of vertical joints, swipe them through the thinset before pushing them into place. The sealed tile makes the cement easy to remove the next day.

Cut a Laminate Countertop for a Sink

BY ANDY ENGEL

When you're building or remodeling a kitchen, you can save time and money by using a ready-made laminate countertop. These tops, which generally have an integral backsplash and wraparound front edge, are durable and easy to find at home centers and lumberyards. Even if you have a laminate top custom-fabricated or you make it yourself, you can still use the sink-cutting methods described here.

Many sinks come with a layout template that makes marking the cut easy; you just trace the template with a pencil and cut out the hole with a jigsaw. If you don't have a template, trace around the sink rim with a pencil, and then adjust the line inward to get the proper fit. On dark tops like this one, I make the layout marks on light-colored masking tape so they're easier to see.

I cut most of the opening with a jigsaw equipped with a laminate-cutting blade. These blades cut on the downstroke to prevent chipping. If the countertop has an integral backsplash, there's usually not enough room for a jigsaw when making the rear cut (adjacent to the backsplash). I make this cut with an oscillating multitool.

After making the rear cut, I attach a cleat to the cutout with a single screw. The cleat supports the cutout in place to prevent the countertop from

CENTER THE SINK. Use a combination square lined up between the cabinet doors to establish the side-to-side location of the sink. Make sure the front cut won't hit the cabinet rail below.

breaking as the cut is finished. I use one screw so I can rotate the cleat out of the blade's path while cutting.

To make less mess, you might be tempted to cut the top outdoors or in your shop and then move the prepared top to the sink base. I generally don't do this because with a large hole in the center, it's very easy to break the countertop while moving it.

MAKE THE CUT

To prevent damaging the laminate countertop, use a reverse-cutting jigsaw blade. These blades have teeth that cut on the downstroke instead of the upstroke. Go slowly, and apply steady downward pressure so that the saw doesn't bounce while cutting.

There's often not enough room to fit a jigsaw between the back of the sink and the backsplash. In these instances, use a fine-tooth blade in an oscillating multitool. Make the cut in several passes so you don't overheat the blade, which slows cutting and dulls the teeth.

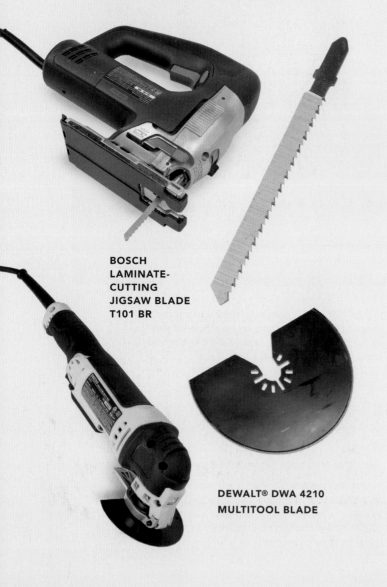

BOSCH LAMINATE-CUTTING JIGSAW BLADE T101 BR

DEWALT® DWA 4210 MULTITOOL BLADE

TRACE THE LINE. Trace the template or the sink rim as the starting point for layout lines. A layer of tape helps you see the pencil lines.

DOUBLE-CHECK THE LAYOUT. Confirm that the cuts will be covered fully by the sink rim, then cross out the original lines to prevent cutting on the wrong line.

ATTACH A CLEAT. To prevent the top from breaking as you finish the cut, secure a cleat to the top. A single screw in the center allows you to rotate the cleat out of the way while cutting.

MOVE THE LINE INWARD. Without a template, the layout line must be moved inward so it will be covered by the sink rim. The margins vary by sink, but the minimum is about ¼ in. Make a mark at both ends of all four sides.

CONNECT THE DOTS. Use a straightedge to connect the marks that correspond with the actual cutline. Connect the corners at an angle for an easier cut and better sink support.

DRILL THE CORNERS. Drill the insides of every corner with a ⅜-in. spade bit. Make sure the holes are fully within the lines that mark the actual sink cutout.

CUT THE BACK. Because of the backsplash, there's generally not enough room to cut the back side with a jigsaw. Instead, use a fine-tooth blade in an oscillating multitool.

FINISH UP WITH A JIGSAW. Use a jigsaw with a reverse-cutting blade to finish the sink cutout. Maintain downward pressure to keep the saw from bouncing as it cuts.

TEST THE FIT. After checking that the sink fits inside the cutout, clean all dust from the countertop, run a bead of silicone sealant around the rim, and install the clips that secure the sink.

EDGES. A powerful orbital sander known as an edger sands the flooring around the edges of each room and in any areas too small to be handled by the full-size belt sander.

LARGE AREAS. Heavy, powerful, and aggressive, a professional-grade belt sander (which can be rented) does the heaviest lifting in a floor-refinishing job. Slow, overlapping passes are made in the direction of the floorboards.

CORNERS. Scraping with a handheld draw scraper followed by some hand sanding quickly reveals bare wood in corners and around details where a sander won't fit. Wherever the scraper goes, so does a metal file, which is used frequently to hone the scraper's cutting edge.

GET BACK TO BARE WOOD. The first pass with the belt sander and the edger, which we call the rough cut, typically relies on 36-grit paper to remove the existing finish and stain quickly, revealing fresh wood across most of the floor.

Refinish Your Wood Floors

BY BRENT KELOSKY

Although my company does all types of flooring installations, our bread and butter has always been refinishing worn hardwood. Our goal is to uncover the beauty under the decrepit surface of the floor, which involves no small amount of labor.

When we arrived on-site for the job shown here, the wall-to-wall carpeting had already been removed, revealing 750 sq. ft. of severely worn red-oak flooring that appeared original to this old Pennsylvania farmhouse. Although we got back down to bare wood quickly, that's just the beginning of a job like this.

The job took a two-person crew just under five days to complete and cost about $4.50 per sq. ft. in labor and materials. Refinishing a hardwood floor is an admittedly disruptive process, but you realize it's worth it when you first set eyes on the results.

The materials are straightforward—just a single coat of stain, a coat of sealer to lock in the stain, and two coats of polyurethane to provide the wear layer—but breathing new life into an old wood floor takes a lot of patience. It all starts with sanding.

Sanding Will Make or Break Your Job

Without question, the critical difference between a professional-looking finished floor and a poor attempt is how much care is taken during the sanding stage. Although you're only removing $1/16$ in. or so of actual wood, the sanding process takes multiple days—that is, if it's done correctly.

In addition to some common hand and power tools, there are three specialized tools we use on our jobs: a belt floor sander, an orbital edger, and a buffer.

The bulk of the sanding work is handled by the large, very aggressive, 220v belt sander. Run back and forth through the room, working in the same direction as the floor's wood grain, the belt sander is used to take slow, overlapping passes.

Although an upright orbital sander is the most common tool available at rental yards, we prefer to use a belt sander. (A drum sander is also an improvement over the orbital.) An orbital sander is a fairly gentle and forgiving tool, which may seem appealing if you're unsure of your abilities, but it also requires much more time to do the job. On badly damaged floors, you'll likely give up long before you get the blemishes sanded out.

A belt sander runs on wheels and uses a lever to lower the machine—which puts the sanding belt in contact with the floor surface—and then to lift it away. Because the machine is so aggressive, you can't allow it to sit in one spot for even a couple of

DEALING WITH DAMAGE

WE OFTEN SEE PET STAINS, traffic patterns, knife marks along the edges of the room left from the carpet installation, and missing wood or abandoned registers. Our first choice is always to sand out the damage if we can, but damage often extends beyond the missing, scratched, or dented wood.

Sanding can't fix everything, and often it's impossible to predict whether a damaged section can be sanded out until you try. For areas that can't be remedied with sanding, there are two options: acceptance or board replacement.

When sanding damaged areas, we take several passes with the belt sander at a slight angle to the wood grain, alternating the angle of the machine between each series of passes. It sometimes helps to spray the surface of the damaged flooring with water—just enough to wet it evenly—between passes with the belt sander. The water raises the grain of the wood, lifting deeper stains to be within reach of the sander.

We typically don't bother filling large gaps with putty. Experience has taught us that the camouflage rarely lasts and that this repair isn't worth the effort. It's extremely difficult to fill an entire void, and seasonal movement combined with vibrations of walking usually open the gaps again. These imperfections are often best left as they are.

seconds or you will end up with significant gouges. It should be lowered to the floor as it's being moved forward to start a pass, then lifted back off at the end of each pass.

A powerful handheld orbital sander called an edger is used to sand the perimeter of the room and any areas where the larger machine won't fit. The smallest details and corners are done by hand with a scraper and sandpaper. Later in the process, a buffing machine is outfitted for finer sanding, but first comes the rough cut.

Sand Incrementally and Patiently

Although it's not the coarsest option in our arsenal, 24-grit is typically the lowest grit we use for the rough cut. Such a coarse grit is only necessary when a floor has lots of built-up wax on the surface, and even then it's pretty inefficient for removing actual wood. In most cases, we start with 36-grit sandpaper, which removes the existing topcoats

TRACK YOUR PROGRESS. Although the sanding progress isn't as dramatic as during the rough cut, the incremental passes with belt sander, edger, buffer, and random-orbit sander are crucial and demand a slow, methodical system. To ensure that no spots are skipped, use a hard piece of rubber to mark across the grain of the floor before sanding. Rubber is more reliable than a marker, which can dry out quickly.

BACK IT UP ONE GRIT. Use a random-orbit sander to retouch the edges of the room. Although the rest of the floor is sanded to 80-grit, use 60-grit paper here to avoid a halo effect around the room's perimeter.

BUFF TO BLEND. The final sanding pass is done with a buffer that's equipped with a multidisk head and 80-grit paper. This setup blends the scratch patterns of the belt sander and the edger, ensuring a uniform look when stain is applied.

USE THE FLOOR AS THE SAMPLE BOARD. The most accurate way to decide between stain colors is to apply the stain options right to the floor after the first or second pass with the belt sander. They can then be sanded out with the next pass.

and stain, revealing fresh wood across most of the floor. From there, we sand the floor twice more with 50-grit and 80-grit paper, spending additional time on problem areas such as deep scratches or surface stains (see "Dealing with Damage," facing page).

A crucial step that's often not considered by first-timers is blending together the sanding patterns from the belt sander and the edger. Because they have different weights, operate at different speeds, and are run in different directions, these two machines leave the sanded floor looking and feeling inconsistent, even when they're equipped with the same grit of sandpaper. The remedy for this problem is a random-orbit sander.

Even though we use 80-grit paper with the belt sander and the edger, experience has taught us that the random-orbit sander should be equipped with 60-grit paper, which roughs up the perimeter of the room and any other areas where the two machines had overlapping passes. Although it seems counterintuitive, this ensures that the stain penetrates evenly. A final pass with the upright buffer machine is the last step in the sanding process before the floor undergoes a thorough vacuuming.

Staining Is Done by Hand

Although water-based stains are an option, I've found them to be inferior to oil-based products,

A TWO-PERSON STAINING TEAM. When working in large, open areas, the fastest option is to apply the oil-based stain using a pad on the buffer machine. But for most jobs, the best way to apply stain is also the most labor-intensive: wiping it on by hand. Working on padded hands and knees to prevent moisture spots that will keep the stain from penetrating evenly, the first person wipes the stain on using a folded cotton cloth while the second person follows behind, using another cloth to work the stain into the wood in a firm, circular rubbing motion.

especially in getting even stain color in large rooms. Along with the sealer and topcoats that come after it, we use stain from Bona Kemi. When using multiple cans of stain, we combine them in one bucket to ensure that the color is uniform. We apply the stain with a lint-free cloth, then wipe the excess before it dries in place.

It's critical to protect the unstained portions of the floor from moisture as you work. Water in the wood causes that part of the floor to absorb pigment differently, and even something as subtle as perspiration through the knees of your pants can leave discolored blotches in the finished floor. Always use disposable shoe covers when you're walking the floor; bare or socked feet are an absolute no. Kneepads are essential, as well as a rag under each hand. In hot weather, a cloth tied around the head will catch sweat dripping from your brow.

Sandpaper scratches that went unnoticed during the previous floor-prep phase often become obvious as they trap pigment during the stain application. These scratches can be sanded by hand with the same 80-grit paper used in the last pass of the sanders and then recoated right away with stain. There's no need to bother with the vacuum.

When the schedule allows, we like to let the stain dry overnight. If the sealer will be applied later the

TOPCOATS SHARE THE SAME TECHNIQUE. The topcoats on a floor—from the single coat of sealer through the two coats of water-based polyurethane—are applied using the same tools and techniques. Make sure to buff the floor after the seal coat, but you shouldn't need to sand between or after the coats of polyurethane. The edges come first. Working just ahead of the person applying finish with the T-bar, coat the perimeter of the room by pouring a thin line of finish directly onto the floor, then spread it with a handheld applicator pad.

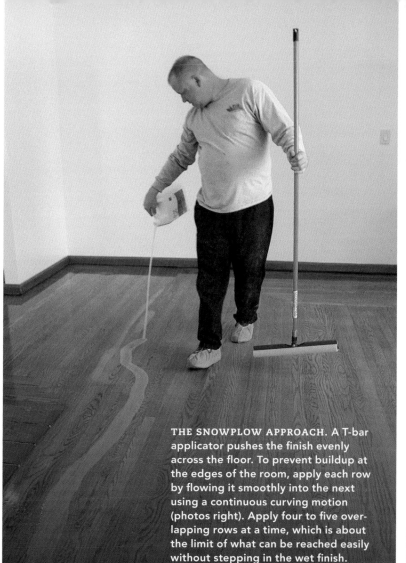

THE SNOWPLOW APPROACH. A T-bar applicator pushes the finish evenly across the floor. To prevent buildup at the edges of the room, apply each row by flowing it smoothly into the next using a continuous curving motion (photos right). Apply four to five overlapping rows at a time, which is about the limit of what can be reached easily without stepping in the wet finish.

same day, we check for dryness by wiping a white cotton cloth across the stained surface. If no stain is transferred to the cloth, it's dry enough to move on to the seal coat, which is a waterborne product used to separate the stain from the topcoats that come next. Depending on the brand of polyurethane, the sealer may not be a strict prerequisite, but we use it to provide an extra layer of build above the stain, which enhances the visual depth of the topcoats. After the sealer dries, minor blemishes and nail holes can be filled with a putty that matches the

RETOUCH THE CURVES. Remove the perimeter curve marks by feathering the finish from the edges of the room inward, wringing excess from the T-bar by pressing it firmly on the unfinished part of the floor.

SMOOTH THE SEAL COAT. Supplement a maroon (very fine grit) buffing pad with strips of 180-grit adhesive sandpaper to smooth out the dried coat of sealer, being careful not to walk on buffed surfaces.

stain color before the entire floor is abraded with the buffer. Then the floor gets another pass with the vacuum, followed by a pass with tack cloths to pick up any remaining dust.

Waterborne Polyurethane Is the Most Durable Choice

Although we use oil-based stain, we switch to a waterborne product for the polyurethane topcoats because the waterborne products have lower odor and faster dry times and are actually more durable than oil-based topcoats. For sheen, I encourage customers to opt for either satin or semigloss, because wear patterns from pets and foot traffic are more obvious on floors with high-gloss finishes.

A small handheld foam pad is used to apply the polyurethane around the perimeter of the room, around details such as balusters and hearths, and in small areas. While the edges and details are still wet, a T-bar with a spongy applicator pad spreads finish across the rest of the floor in rows that follow the direction of the grain.

Optimum conditions for drying the topcoat are temperatures between 65°F and 80°F, with 40% to 60% relative humidity and some air movement to help wick away moisture, but not so much that it blows dust around.

PUSH-BROOM TACK CLOTH. After sanding the seal coat and vacuuming the floors, put on shoe covers and pick up the last bits of dust with a moistened towel wrapped around the head of a push broom (above). This ensures a clean surface for the first coat of polyurethane (top).

The coat of sealer and the first coat of polyurethane are typically dry enough for a recoating in about 4 hours, but we never apply more than two coats of finish in a single day. My advice here is not to rush it, because the most recent coat of finish always dries faster than what's under it, and you don't want to risk trapping moisture, which leads to adhesion problems.

There should be no need for sanding between or after coats of polyurethane. After the last coat, the floor can be walked on gently in about 4 or 5 hours, but restrict normal foot traffic for 24 hours. Anything that might prevent drying, such as an area rug, shouldn't be replaced until after seven days to allow the finish to cure fully.

Install Wood Floors on a Concrete Slab

BY KEVIN WARD

Here in Texas, as in much of the South and West, houses are built on concrete slabs. For a flooring contractor like me, a slab can be a mixed blessing. Concrete is stable, doesn't bounce, and won't expand or contract seasonally like wood. However, it does limit the clients' choices for wood-flooring installations. Obviously, you can't use nails to attach the flooring. The advent of engineered flooring (hardwood veneer glued to a plywood substrate) made the choice of hardwood on a slab an easy one. Glued down with a urethane adhesive, engineered flooring doesn't move in service as much as solid wood, is easy to install with the right prep work, and looks great for years.

There are a few tricks to a successful installation, and in this case, preparation is more than half the job. Recently, my company was contracted to install more than 1,000 sq. ft. of reclaimed-oak engineered flooring of random widths in a new house outside of Austin, and the job provided a good example of how we work.

MOISTURE METERS

ON THIS JOB, THE ENGINEERED flooring's plywood construction isn't particularly susceptible to seasonal changes, but we test the product anyway to make sure its moisture content is less than 10%. I've found that the Mini-Ligno® E/D (Lignomat) is portable and accurate. Concrete's density and lower moisture levels require a separate meter, and I use a Tramex® CME 4, a pinless meter that lets me take a number of accurate readings quickly.

Ensure the Substrate Is Flat and Dry

Before the job starts, I go to the site and check the slab's moisture content. There are a couple of different methods for doing this, but the easiest and most accurate is to use a moisture meter. The slab's moisture content should register about 4% or less. If you're working with a new slab, it's a good idea to allow it to cure for at least 90 days before checking its moisture content. If the slab is too wet, the

CHECK FOR FLATNESS. A glue-down floor must be installed on a slab that has less than a ³⁄₁₆-in. deviation in level over 10 ft. The slab must also be at the proper height so that the transitions are smooth between flooring and adjacent tiles, doorways, and stairs. Examine the entire slab with a long straightedge (at least 10 ft. is preferable), and mark high and low areas with a pencil.

FLATTEN THE HIGH SPOTS. Use a rotary hammer or angle grinder to grind down high spots, periodically checking progress with a straightedge. Afterward, sweep and vacuum the area.

PRIME THE LOW SPOTS. Before the low areas can be filled, the slab surface must be abraded with a buffer and 36-grit sandpaper, then painted with an acrylic bonding agent.

MAKE IT FLOW. Mix the self-leveling compound, pour it onto a low area, and use a long straightedge as a screed to smooth its surface. Blend the edges into the slab with a trowel.

DRY-FIT THE FIRST PIECES. Because the flooring must fit under the cut door jambs and around jogs in the walls, dry-fit those pieces, then check to make sure that they are parallel to the chalkline.

START SPREADING THE GLUE. After fitting and gluing the scribed areas in the hallway, use a 3/16-in. V-notch trowel to spread the adhesive between the chalklines of the starter.

TO AVOID ACCUMULATED ERRORS, START THE LAYOUT IN THE MIDDLE OF THE ROOM AND WORK TOWARD THE WALLS. In this house, the central hallway determined the location of the starter row. After snapping two lines about 2 ft. apart and parallel to both walls, dry-fit areas that need to be scribed, then begin installation. Painter's tape and buckets of sand keep the glued starter row in place.

STAY BETWEEN THE LINES. Push the first course of flooring into the adhesive, and check to see that it's aligned with the chalkline. A couple of hammer taps help to set the pieces. As you fill in the rest of the starter, make sure the flooring isn't wandering over the line.

WORK TOWARD THE WALLS. With the starter row established, continue the installation in one direction in increments approximately 2 ft. wide. Within a couple of courses' width of the wall, dry-fit the last course against the wall, then glue it down. Repeat the process on the opposite side of the room.

flooring adhesive won't bond properly. Alternatively, you can use either a moisture-barrier membrane that's applied before the adhesive or a moisture-barrier/adhesive combination. (These alternatives are available from many manufacturers, but they cost twice as much as the simple adhesive process.) Even if I know the slab is dry, I always check and record the moisture reading in case something goes wrong later.

Next, I use razor scrapers to clean accumulated paint, dirt, and gunk off the slab. Then I sweep and vacuum it clean so that nothing interferes when I check the slab's flatness.

I use a 10-ft.-long aluminum straightedge to find the high and low spots on the floor. Doorways, transitions, and floor outlets are the serial offenders here.

I grind down the high spots, checking with a straightedge as I go. I use a flooring buffer to scuff up the low areas. While I'm scuffing, one of my crew

HIDE CUT EDGES. Whenever I crosscut a piece of prefinished flooring, I knock off any fuzz from the cut end and then give it a quick swipe with the proper stain so the cut edge won't show.

ADJUST WIDTH WITH A RABBET PLANE. Occasionally, a board that's 1/16 in. or so wider than its nominal width gets installed. Rather than pull it out, it's sometimes easier to use a rabbet plane (I like the Stanley® No. 92) to gradually reduce the excess width over the length of the piece.

ALWAYS DRY-FIT TRICKY AREAS. Flooring must be scribed to fit around floor outlets, doorways, and walls that aren't parallel. Double-check measurements, then try a dry fit before gluing. Always leave a 3/16-in. gap around the perimeter of the room. To scribe the last row of flooring, begin by aligning the piece to be scribed to the previous row.

is mixing self-leveling compound in a 5-gal. bucket. The compound's consistency must be liquid enough to seek its own level but stiff enough not to run across the floor.

After vacuuming and applying a polymer bonding agent to the low areas to be filled, I screed the leveling compound, trowel the edges into the slab surface, and let it dry overnight.

The next day, I use the buffer again to flatten any ridges in the compound. After a good vacuuming, I protect any finished surfaces close to the floor with painter's tape. At this stage, I also use an oscillating multitool and a scrap of flooring as a gauge to undercut door casings, cabinet stiles, and kicks so that the flooring has plenty of clearance.

Establish a Starter Row

The best way to start the installation is to create a starter row that's about 2 ft. wide and that runs across the entire room. I like to establish the starter row near the center of the room so that I can adjust in both directions. After measuring the space, I snap a chalkline along the long axis and check to see if it is parallel to each wall. A second line about 2 ft. from the first gives us the limits of the starter row.

SCRIBE THE LINE. Holding a short scrap of flooring (under 12 in.) of the previous row's width against the wall and on top of the piece to be scribed, trace its edge. Repeat along the wall until you've scribed the line along the entire piece.

Before spreading any glue, I fit the flooring to the doorways and bump-outs in the hall. It's important not to apply more glue than can be covered in about 40 minutes, the average working time for the urethane adhesive. Once the glue is applied, you only want to put the flooring down once. It's critical that the starter row remain straight, so check the distance to the chalkline after fitting a piece.

RIP AND FIT. After ripping the piece at the pencil line, test the fit, then spread the glue and drop the piece in. The width of the tongue on the scrap piece creates the 3/16-in. gap at the wall.

SQUEEZE IT IN. Use a flat bar to lever the last piece into place. A scrap of flooring used as a backer prevents the bar from damaging the drywall.

I spread the glue with a 3/16-in. V-notch trowel within the chalked lines. (To set the starter on this job, I wanted at least 20 ft. of length.) I lay the flooring onto the glue, aligning it to the chalkline and staggering the joints at least 12 in. between courses. A few taps with a rubber mallet help to push each board into the glue. With three courses down, I stretch a piece of painter's tape across the row every couple of feet to help hold the boards together.

After checking to see that the starter row is on the line and parallel to the walls, I weigh it down with 5-gal. buckets filled with sand and let the adhesive cure overnight.

Switch to production mode

The next day, I measure out about 2 ft. from the starter courses, snap a chalkline, spread the glue, and lay down the flooring as before. I repeat this sequence to within two or three courses of the wall.

Because the last course must be fit to the wall, I scribe, cut, and dry-fit the last course, then apply the adhesive, install the pieces, and bring in the sand buckets.

When the adhesive is dry and the floor is complete, I vacuum and sweep thoroughly until every speck of dirt is picked up. To protect the floor from the next wave of trades, I cover it with a tough, vapor-permeable covering such as Ram Board™ and tape all the seams. I also schedule a day to return and repair any scratches or blemishes, right before the clients are scheduled to move in.

SOURCES

Manufacturers of sealers, adhesives, and self-leveling compounds include the following:

BOSTIK®
www.bostik.com/us

MAPEI®
www.mapei.com

DRITAC®
www.dritac.com

FRANKLIN® ADHESIVES AND POLYMERS
www.franklinadhesivesandpolymers.com

PART 4

Real-World Kitchens

Universal Appeal

BY DEBRA JUDGE SILBER

In Bill and Allison Pileggi's kitchen, it's one cool idea after another: drawers snuck into toe kicks, cabinet doors that slip out of sight, appliances that pop open on command. Then there are the attractive features: the orderly white cabinetry that offers glimpses of colorful dishware through its glass, the marble and granite countertops that weave together in a rectilinear backsplash behind the cooktop. It's a kitchen with broad appeal, even though it was painstakingly designed to meet the family's needs. This kitchen sends a strong message: Universal design is more individual than you might think.

Paralyzed from the waist down since college, Allison uses a wheelchair. While that fact certainly impacts her requirements in a kitchen, it doesn't mean that her needs are the same as those of every other homeowner with mobility issues. "I'm very functional; I bend down to pick up stuff all the time," Allison says when asked about the toe-kick drawers where she stashes everything from towels to plasticware. "For someone else, that might not be an option. That's why universal-design needs are so specific."

Allison and Bill wanted a kitchen matched to their needs and tastes, not to generic ADA standards. The problem was that none of the kitchen designers they consulted grasped this.

A Universal Playbook with Someone Else's Moves

The Pileggis bought their suburban Pittsburgh ranch home because it offered both single-floor accessibility and the potential for improvement, especially in its galley kitchen. It would be eight years, however, before they got around to the kitchen remodel they planned from the start.

In the year leading up to the project, the Pileggis gathered photos of kitchens they liked, investigated appliance options, and churned out design sketches. In these notes and drawings, they discovered a kitchen that would do more than accommodate Allison's reach; it also would provide a comfortable environment for her husband, daughter, and others. "My mom comes on weekends, and I knew she was going to be working in this kitchen," Allison explains, "so I didn't want it specific to my needs." Aesthetics also was important for Allison and Bill. They wanted an attractive, family-friendly kitchen—not, as Bill says, "an occupational-therapy lab."

Their homework complete, the Pileggis consulted local kitchen designers. The plans that they came back with, though, were a disappointment. "We knew what we needed, but we thought a kitchen designer would fill in all the gaps," Bill says. "Each

came back without a clue to what we were asking for. Either their CAD design had no aesthetic quality and looked institutional, or it simply ignored the fact that the person using this kitchen had to do it from a wheelchair."

Allison and Bill decided to take the kitchen design into their own hands, although they still needed professionals to translate their specifications into framing and cabinetry. Those needs were met by New Hampshire-based Crown Point Cabinetry, whose designer, Mike Murphy, spent four months drawing and redrawing plans, and by Nick Cratsa, a local contractor willing to add to the family's vision. The result is a universally comfortable kitchen that blends accessible design with rich materials and fun, family-friendly features. "There's something in this kitchen for everybody," Bill says.

Issues and Invention

The renovation encompassed the original 10-ft. by 22-ft. galley kitchen and adjacent spaces, which included a tight powder room, an entry from the

THE PERFECT MIX. A mixer lift promised to be a big help in the kitchen, but mounting the hardware on the cabinet sides would require a space-hogging swinging door. The answer: A false wall inside the cabinet that also creates a pocket for a retractable door.

back patio, and a laundry/mechanical room at the end of a narrow hallway. The space totaled 440 sq. ft., with a wall dividing the kitchen from the other areas.

After moving the furnace to the attic, the Pileggis looked into moving the wall to widen the kitchen so that it could accommodate an accessible island with at least 3 ft. on all sides. The good news was that the wall, which other contractors had described as load bearing, bore only the ceiling. "Nick sat at the kitchen table with his laptop, and he said, 'You have nothing above you. Have you thought about raising the ceiling?' " Bill recalls. Allison still wanted the cabinets to connect with a flat ceiling, so they devised a hybrid tray and vaulted ceiling, with a skylight where the 5-ft.-tall attic space had been.

With the old laundry-room hallway absorbed by the new powder room, laundry-room access was moved to the kitchen. Allison and Bill didn't want

BEFORE

The original galley kitchen wasn't wide enough to accommodate an island, and the adjacent laundry/mechanical room could be accessed only by a narrow hallway. Access to the small powder room also was not ideal.

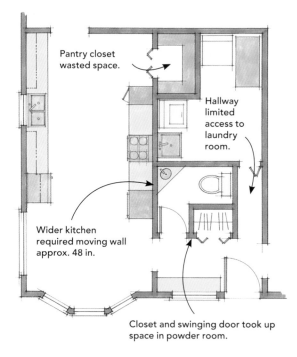

Pantry closet wasted space.

Hallway limited access to laundry room.

Wider kitchen required moving wall approx. 48 in.

Closet and swinging door took up space in powder room.

AFTER

Moving the kitchen wall, which supported the original flat ceiling, not only provided the family with room for an island, but also allowed them to open the space above with a vaulted tray ceiling and a skylight. Laundry-room access was made through the kitchen, and the dysfunctional hallway was incorporated into a larger powder room. Outfitted with new cabinetry, electrical, and plumbing, the kitchen was ready to accommodate a wealth of accessible and functional features.

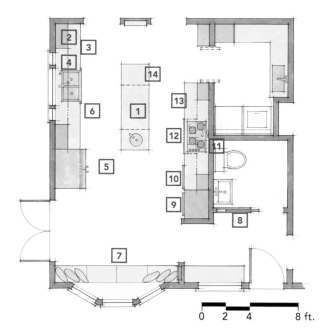

0   2   4   8 ft.

to interrupt the line of cabinetry on that side with a doorway, but they also knew that any door flush with the cabinets would have to swing out, creating an impassable location. The answer lay in hardware from the cabinetmaker that enabled a pair of tall cabinet-style doors to swing open and then slide backward. With the doors retracted, the 28-in. pass-through is just wide enough for Allison's wheelchair. "It's amazing how an inch here and an inch there makes a difference," Bill says.

"If You Can Draw It, We Can Make It"

With space concerns addressed, it was clear the dark, outdated cabinets and appliances had to go. "I was very interested in having an off-white kitchen with inset cabinet doors," Allison says. The desire for this style led her to Crown Point, but more than the cabinets sold her. "They were the ones who said, 'If you can draw it, we can make it,' " she says.

1. Accessible island measures 84 in. long by 27 in. wide by 30 in. high.
2. Deeper wall cabinets shorten reach to shelves; appliance garages extend storage to countertop.
3. Dishwasher drawer
4. Window counter height of 34½ in. enables views outside.
5. 45 in. of space on each side of island
6. Toe kicks 7 in. high accommodate Allison's wheelchair but maintain typical kitchen proportions.
7. Pneumatic hinges and small sections make bench storage accessible.
8. Pocket door
9. Easy-to-use ball-bearing oven racks
10. Microwave drawer opens with a touch button.
11. Reachable pot filler
12. 35½-in. cooktop height
13. Refrigerator drawer keeps essentials within reach of everyone.
14. Mixer lift with retractable doors

BLENDING IN. Clearances needed for the Fisher & Paykel® refrigerator drawer dictated the 35½-in. height of the counter on that side of the kitchen. The adjacent laundry-room pantry is accessed through retractable doors that slide forward to close, creating the appearance of an unbroken line of cabinetry.

That began a four-month exchange of more than 220 emails loaded with dimensions, product suggestions, and scans of pencil sketches and handwritten notes. Mike translated all of this into a design scheme in Cabinet Vision®, the software his company uses. "Mike was like the engineer," says Bill. "It was so collaborative, it was beautiful."

What did Mike get that other designers didn't? His answer seems too simple. "It comes down to just listening closely to what it is they're trying to achieve, and putting myself in their place," he says.

For Allison, one of those things was a cabinet finish that not only would brighten the kitchen but also would hold up to occasional dings from a wheelchair. Mike sent samples of each finish for Allison to test. She opted for a painted finish that

could be touched up easily. Other features important to the couple included lots of drawers, which are easier to access for everyone, and countertop heights ranging from 30 in. on the island to 35½ in. at the cooktop. A new window behind the sink is about 5 in. lower than the original, enabling Allison—and 7-year-old daughter Lila—to look into the yard and the retired apple orchard beyond.

The stainless-steel farmhouse sink protrudes from the cabinet base by about 1½ in., offering a wide ledge that Allison can grip when reaching for the faucet. A pot filler over the stove enables her to fill pasta pots at the point of use. A mixer lift in the island was designed to accommodate retractable doors, and storage drawers fill most of the kitchen's 7-in. toe-kick space. This recess, 2 in. shorter than

OVEN OPTIONS. While a side-opening oven might be considered more accessible, the Pileggis liked the features of this Thermador, including the ball-bearing slides that help racks to move in and out easily.

toe kicks typically recommended for accessible kitchens, is high enough to accommodate the footrests on Allison's wheelchair without throwing off the aesthetic balance of the cabinetry. "ADA standards are terrific, but you can manipulate them," says Mike, who has designed a number of universal kitchens, including one for a former football player. "Not every person is the same size; not every wheelchair is the same width."

In fact, the Pileggis have discovered that the kitchen's proportions are ideal for all its frequent cooks. "My mom is only about five-one, so the lower countertop works for her," Allison says. "Anyone who has worked in this kitchen has felt

that it really works well." That includes her brother, who is 6 ft. tall.

Appliance Approach

"We really scrutinized the appliances," says Bill, who made outfitting the kitchen his personal mission. Prize finds included a Thermador wall oven and steam oven. The controls are placed between them within easy reach, and the ball-bearing slides on the lower ovens' racks ease access. The paneled refrigerator has a freezer on the bottom, but refrigerator items Allison can't reach are stocked in a refrigerated drawer. The microwave, mounted in the base cabinet to the right of the cooktop, and the dishwasher both are drawer models. The cooktop

CALCULATED MOVE. Before cabinets were installed, contractor Nick Cratsa drew a line on the wall to mark the countertop height, then asked Allison to test her reach before he positioned the pot filler.

SOURCES

CABINETRY
Crown Point Cabinetry
www.crown-point.com

**DISHWASHER AND
REFRIGERATOR DRAWER**
Fisher & Paykel
www.fisherpaykel.com

MICROWAVE DRAWER
Sharp®
www.sharpusa.com

MIXER LIFT
Knape & Vogt
www.knapeandvogt.com

SINK
Kräus®
www.kraususa.com

WALL AND STEAM OVENS
Thermador
www.thermador.com

is induction. Its cool-to-the-touch surface was not a necessity, Allison says, but she admits, "I do lean over it. And having a young daughter—it's safer for her, too."

What Made It Work

Bill and Allison say that it was their contractor's and cabinetmaker's open-mindedness and willingness to collaborate that got them the kitchen they wanted. Nick and Mike say that it was also the enormous time and effort the Pileggis put into analyzing and then clearly communicating their needs. "What was great about working with Bill and Allison is they knew exactly what they wanted," says Nick.

Mike agrees: "They had their ducks in a row," he said. "They prepared for quite some time, and it shows."

Surgical Kitchen Remodel

BY DAVID GETTS

The key to a successful small remodeling project is to make the new work match the existing details so that no one can tell that the space was ever modified. On this job, upgrading the double ovens in an existing kitchen meant that I had to create a little more room in a run of the 20-year-old cabinets for a new, larger oven cabinet, and then make everything look as though it had been built that way. The job was complicated because I had to modify the granite counter and base cabinet in place. It was more like kitchen surgery than remodeling.

My plan was to remove the ovens and the oven cabinet, as well as the upper cabinet to the right and the drawers below it, then to resize the upper cabinet and cut 3 in. from the counter and face frame below. If I worked carefully, the new oven cabinet would fit like a glove in the newly expanded space.

Ovens Out, Electrical In

First, I protected the area by taping down Ram Board on the floor, setting up ZipWall® barriers in doorways, and taping 4-mil plastic over all the cabinets. I also checked the electrical requirements before the work began. Two new circuits were

BEFORE

AFTER

REMODELING BY THE INCH.
The existing ovens were tired
and ready to go. The problem was that they were 27 in.
wide, while most new ovens
are 30 in. wide. Rather than
struggle to find the same size,
my client, Ginger, decided that
she wanted the larger oven,
which meant enlarging the
space by 3 in. for the appliance
cabinet. This cabinet occupied
the center of one wall in her
fairly small kitchen. To preserve
working counter space, it made
the most sense to expand the
cabinet space in one direction
toward the inside corner rather
than toward the cooktop. The
move in that direction also
would help to minimize any
visual impact of the remodel.

needed, and fortunately there was a subpanel in the
kitchen area that I could easily tap into. This made
it a one-day rough-in for the electrician. If we had
needed to run the circuit from the main house panel,
I would have had the electrician run it into the attic
space above the kitchen before the demolition began
to minimize any disruption to the homeowner.

Next, I removed the existing ovens and cut apart
the cabinet to make them easier to pull out. After the

electrician roughed in the new outlets, I patched and
primed the drywall behind the cabinets.

Cutting a Granite Counter in Place

If the countertop had been short, I would have
pulled it out and had it cut off site. Because the
countertop extended around a corner, though,
I thought that removing it was too risky. If the

THE EASY UPPER. Because it didn't support the counter, the adjacent upper cabinet was simply unscrewed and brought back to the shop for resizing.

BACKSPLASH SURGERY. A multitool was the first choice to remove backsplash tile in the footprint of the new cabinet. It was much easier to remove full courses of tile and then replace the missing partials after the new cabinet was installed.

REMOVE IN PIECES. To avoid harming the neighboring cabinets, the author took apart the oven cabinet with reciprocating and circular saws.

NO MISTAKES HERE. The counter was cut carefully with an angle grinder fitted with a diamond blade. The nozzle of the job-site vacuum was positioned at the blade to capture as much dust as possible. The crew also wore dust masks and protective eyewear.

FOLLOW THE GUIDE. To trim the lower cabinet's face frame, the author screwed a straightedge to the face-frame stile, then made the cuts with a small circular saw fitted with a 40-tooth carbide blade to minimize tearout. A multitool took care of the hard-to-get areas.

REPEAT AS NECESSARY. After the face frame had been trimmed, the author used the same technique to trim the cabinet side and back.

counter broke, it would be impossible to find a slab that matched.

I hired a granite fabricator, who arrived with an angle grinder fitted with a diamond blade. I thought he would use a saw and straightedge guide, but he was more comfortable cutting the joint by hand. He drew his mark on a strip of painters' tape and carefully cut along the line. Another method would

have been to use a small circular saw and an edge guide, but the final couple of inches would still have had to be cut with an angle grinder or a similar tool.

Reducing the Cabinets' Width

Of the two cabinets to be modified and reused, the upper was easier. I unscrewed it from the wall and took it back to my shop, where I used a tablesaw, a small circular saw, and a straightedge to cut it down. Because the base cabinet was supporting the

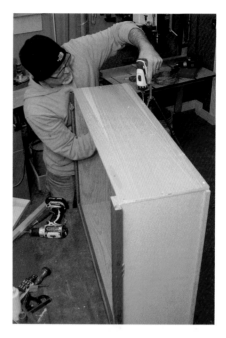

SLOWER FOR SAFETY'S SAKE. Both the upper cabinet and drawers were cut down with the same techniques. After placing the drawer on its bottom and ripping it on a tablesaw, the author used a straightedge guide and a cordless circular saw to cut the narrower ends.

JOINERY OF CONVENIENCE. Rather than try to reproduce the drawers' dovetail joinery, the author trimmed the drawer side and used tapered wooden dowels to join the butt joints.

HERE, THE INTERIOR MATTERS MOST. The new oak plywood side joined to the newly resized upper cabinet had to be finished only on the inside; the exterior is concealed by the adjacent oven cabinet.

countertop, I left it in place and did the modification on site.

The most important aspect of field surgery is getting good, clean cuts so that the new work fits tight in the space. After applying painters' tape to minimize the tearout, I drew the layout in permanent marker.

I also consulted with the finisher before I started doing any modifications. On his advice, I avoided sanding, which meant that I had to be careful to align the new faces as flush as possible. Fortunately, all of the joints either were on the hinge side of the doors or were concealed behind the drawer faces, so any minor discrepancies were not noticeable.

Before any site work began, I built the oven cabinet so that it would be ready to install as soon as we needed it. One thing to keep in mind when building cabinetry for appliances is to follow the manufacturer's requirements, both for safety and

for the warranty. The Miele appliances I installed here had specific venting requirements that led me to build the cabinet without a back and with open airflow throughout the height of the box.

After cutting down the upper cabinet, I attached a new side panel with biscuits and screws. I also reduced the width of the four drawers, making sure that the reassembled part of each drawer was on the side that was obscured when it was opened. The hardest, most labor-intensive part of the job was making the new oven-cabinet doors and a resized door for the adjacent cabinet. I built the cherry doors with a cope-and-stick frame and raised panel that had an uncommon radiused profile.

Reassembly on Site

Back from the shop, I prepped the flanking cabinets first. On the drawer bank, I added a new side. Above,

PREP THE OVEN BASE. The new ovens needed a sturdy, level base, so the author reinforced the existing base with layers of plywood screwed and glued together and shimmed level.

ATTACH THE LOWER SIDE PANEL. Because both faces of the new side would be concealed, the author mounted unfinished AC plywood to the cabinet with pocket screws.

BISCUITS INSTEAD OF NAILS. The cleanest, fastest way to attach the new face-frame stile was to use biscuits and glue. The author cut slots in place, then transferred their positions to the stile.

WORKING SOLO EFFICIENTLY. The rebuilt upper cabinet was installed with the aid of a cabinet jack (Fast Cap®), which held it in place until the mounting screws were driven.

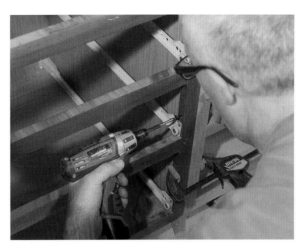

NOT MUCH WIGGLE ROOM. With the oven cabinet in place, the author screwed it to the left-hand base cabinet (top right). After adding plywood blocking (middle right), the oven cabinet was fastened to the right-hand base cabinet.

I reinstalled the upper cabinet and cut slots in both upper and lower box edges for the biscuits that would attach the face-frame stiles. After rebuilding the oven-cabinet base, I pushed the big new cabinet into place, screwed it to the adjacent upper and base cabinets, and then biscuited the face-frame stiles into position.

After the drawer fronts and doors were installed, finisher Rick Fleming formulated a two-step stain process to match the existing finish. The first coat was a water-based aniline dye, followed by an oil stain and a clear topcoat, all of which he applied on site.

THE EXACT WIDTH. It was easier to fit the new right-hand stiles with the oven cabinet in place. The width of the stile was established by the distance between the oven cabinet and the drawer base rails. The author planed the stile to fit precisely.

MATCHING IS PARA-MOUNT. Like everything else on this job, the crown-molding profile was not stock, so the author had to re-create a section of the crown to blend in with the old.

YOU HAVE TO BE THERE. Because a room's mix of natural and artificial light is unique, the finisher's best bet is to try various shades on site. Here, a water-based dye was followed by an oil-based stain and a clear coat of polyurethane.

Kitchen, Meet Dining Room

BY NICOLE STARNES TAYLOR

Old homes are seductive. They charm us with their high ceilings, quiet plaster walls, solid-oak floors, painted wood trim, and scale and proportion that for many of us says "home." I think this is why so many century-old homes in Seattle, where I work, have dodged the wrecking ball and continue to be patched, remodeled, and loved. The one consistent albatross in these sweet old homes, however, is the kitchen.

The floor plan in this 1926 house was typical for the era, with the living room, dining room, and kitchen all stacked along one side of the house.

BEFORE

REMOVING WALLS UNCRAMPS TWO ROOMS. With no increase in the footprint, a small kitchen (photo p. 163) and dining room are now larger and more open. A new half-wall defines the spaces and the new circulation pattern (photo facing page).

The existing kitchen and dining room were each large enough, but they were disconnected from each other through a maze of doors and awkward circulation paths that wasted 75% of the potentially useful space.

My client loves to cook and entertain, so the redesign she hired me for needed to transform her isolated kitchen into the heart of the house. In fact, the new design focused primarily on the kitchen, with the additional goals of connecting better to the backyard and creating a more usable dining room.

We could have extended the home's footprint, but the client and I felt that good design could fix the house's issues on a more reasonable budget. This cost-saving measure allowed more money for custom cabinets, wood flooring, countertops, new windows, and appliances.

The Kitchen Didn't Play Well with the Dining Room

In the existing kitchen, the upper cabinets started 12 in. above the countertop, making food prep and small-appliance usage almost impossible. The lighting was poor, and the kitchen needed more natural light. The existing window over the sink looked directly into the neighbor's house. Southern light and views of the backyard and of downtown

Seattle were cropped by a small window and a mudroom. In the existing dining room, the only spot that made sense for a table was in the way of anyone walking between the kitchen and the living room. Plenty of natural light came from two wide 5-ft.-high windows. However, these windows looked directly into the neighbor's bathroom 10 ft. away. Four doors opening into the dining room reinforced the sense of separation between it and the kitchen.

Opening and Joining the Spaces

By knocking down the wall and an unused chimney between the kitchen and the dining room, and by removing the maze of doors, we streamlined circulation and connected the kitchen and the dining room physically and visually. We added half-height walls with columns at their ends on each end of the dining room to maintain the scale and proportion of the house. These walls share light and views while defining the spaces and creating an alcove for the table that's out of the traffic path.

We tore out the mudroom at the back of the kitchen, adding French doors that allow southern light to pour in and that connect the house to the gracious backyard and views of downtown Seattle. A larger casement replaced the window over the

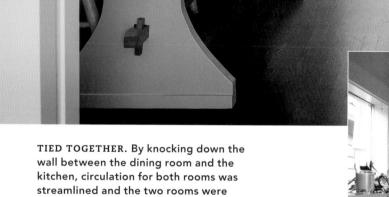

TIED TOGETHER. By knocking down the wall between the dining room and the kitchen, circulation for both rooms was streamlined and the two rooms were tied together physically and visually.

BEFORE

LIGHT AND PRIVACY. The new reeded-glass windows high in the dining-room wall admit daylight but limit the view of the neighboring house. The new half-walls between the rooms create space for the dining table and clearly define the circulation path.

sink. The new window's reeded glass diffuses the view of the neighbor's nearby house.

Where a wall had truncated the kitchen, a peninsula now acts as a perch space. It also slows traffic flow into the kitchen to foster a warm, natural gathering space.

Details Tie the Rooms Together

The existing oak floors in the living room and dining room were carried into the kitchen. The floors' warm, dark-brown stain highlights the painted wood trim. The honed, absolute-black granite countertops define the space, while the subway-tile backsplash with its dark-gray epoxy grout provides a contrasting, softer texture. Vintage light fixtures pay homage to the home's 1920s roots,

while undercabinet lighting provides excellent task lighting at the countertops.

Three new reeded-glass windows high on the dining-room wall bring in light while screening the neighbor's bathroom from sight. General contractor Nicole Dumas built these windows on site. The new pendant fixture above the dining-room table provides a fun, modern focal point to the dining area. Dumas built the table from old-growth fir studs salvaged from demolition.

A beautiful finished project is rewarding for everyone, but it's the process of getting there that makes me want to come to work every morning. For me, that hinges on a strong architect–contractor relationship. In this case, I have known Nicole Dumas for almost a decade, from when we were both carpenters. That field experience developed into an easy rapport and collaborative approach that makes our work more engaging and gives our clients a better process and project.

STOOLS FOR ONLOOKERS. The peninsula provides a spot for guests to sit and chat with the cook. A shelf above the refrigerator keeps cookbooks out of the way, yet accessible.

NEW FLOOR PLAN UNITES EXISTING SPACES

Tearing out existing walls and doors connected the kitchen to the dining room, improving circulation and enlarging the space visually.

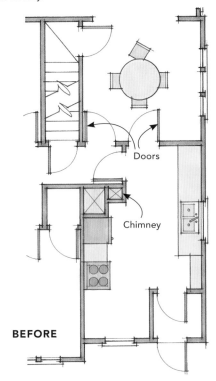

Doors

Chimney

BEFORE

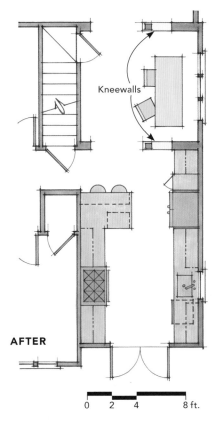

Kneewalls

AFTER

0   2   4   8 ft.

SOURCES

CABINETRY
Pacific Crest®
www.pacificcrest.us

DINING-ROOM FIXTURE
West Elm®
www.westelm.com

FAUCET
Kohler®
www.kohler.com

FRENCH DOOR
Simpson® Door
www.simpsondoor.com

HARDWARE
Restoration Hardware®
www.restorationhardware.com

KITCHEN-CEILING FIXTURE
Rejuvenation® Lighting
www.rejuvenation.com

RANGE
Bertazzoni®
www.bertazzoni.com

REEDED-GLASS CASEMENT
Lindal® Windows
www.lindal.com/windows

TILE
The Home Depot
www.homedepot.com

Tasteful Transformation

BY DAVID O'BRIEN WAGNER

With three growing kids and a family dog, the owners of this 1920s Dutch colonial in the heart of Minneapolis were looking to create a more modern and functional kitchen that would integrate well with the house's traditional bones and detailing. The new kitchen replaces a 1980s remodel and addition that was dark, inefficient, and cramped. The homeowners were interested in creating open and visually connected spaces with a slightly Scandinavian feel as a nod to their family heritage. Budgetary limitations meant that we would be unable to alter the external footprint, so we knew the work would need to be subtle.

Small Changes with Significant Results

The original flow of space from the dining room to the family room was a rat's maze of traffic patterns. The new layout creates a direct route between the front and the back of the house. The new circulation path helps to organize the kitchen into two zones: one for prep and cooking, and the other for cleanup and storage. The original 1980s family room remains unchanged structurally, but we enhanced it with a more focused set of furnished spaces for casual dining and sitting.

BEFORE

BEFORE AND AFTER. A poor 1980s remodel (photo p. 169) is remedied with a new, more logical kitchen layout that's complemented by clean, durable materials and fixtures. Taking a compartmentalized view of the original arrangement of the kitchen and nearby living areas helped the design team reconfigure the kitchen in a way that improves the entire main floor of the home.

AFTER

MEAL PREP. The dual-fuel Wolf range, which anchors the cooking area, sits beneath a modern range hood from Vent-A-Hood® and is flanked by Carrara-marble countertops. The zone is enhanced by extrawide base-cabinet drawers, glass-faced upper cabinets, a continuous marble shelf, and a utensil rack. The design of this zone keeps everything for making a meal within arm's reach, maximizing the efficiency of the small space.

Access to daylight was an important concern for the homeowners, and the kitchen benefits from two new windows. A single Marvin® Magnum double-hung window, with tempered glass in the lower sash, floods the work area with daylight while creating an open, airy atmosphere. A second, smaller window is tucked beneath a set of open shelves to the left of the dishwasher. This small window washes daylight across the countertop while providing an unexpected view to the backyard. The window alcove is framed with the same Carrara marble used for the countertop and nearby shelves.

Light and White

Daylight is generously shared throughout the kitchen by reflecting off the bright marble countertops, walls that are clad in classic white subway tile, and cabinets that have been finished in lustrous off-white enamel paint. The effect is a clean, simple, and timeless style that permeates the kitchen and newly renovated living spaces.

CLEANUP AND STORAGE. The commercially inspired Dornbracht® faucet and Rohl® farmhouse sink are placed directly opposite the range. Base-cabinet drawers, not doors and shelves, provide full and convenient access to most of the kitchen's storage. Additional cabinetry placed on the opposite side of the half-wall that separates the kitchen from the dining area can be used to store collectibles or dining-specific tableware. The entire zone is illuminated with Louis Poulsen® pendants, which impart a distinctly modern quality to the kitchen.

DINING AND ENTERTAINING. The location of the dining room remains unchanged, but from this space, the benefits of the reorganized floor plan are apparent. Long sightlines through the home transform the once dark and contained living areas into an open, light-filled, and comfortable gathering spot. The connectivity between the dining area, the kitchen, and the adjacent living room improves the entire living experience in the home.

3

PLAN CORRECTED

Despite the delineated rooms, the previous layout functioned poorly. By relocating the refrigerator, the architect was able to reconfigure the landing to the basement and simplify the circulation pattern with a direct, open link to the dining and family rooms beyond. The new arrangement revitalized the kitchen and allows views and audible connectivity from space to space.

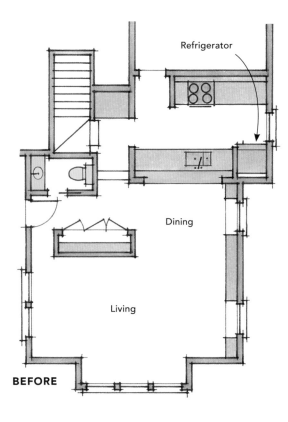

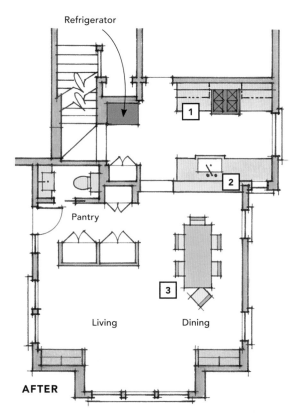

Same Space, Twice the Room

BY NICOLE STARNES TAYLOR

When I first met with Toni-Ann and Neil to discuss their kitchen remodel, I asked them how often they entertain. Their response amazed me. Even with full-time jobs, they cook for family and friends five nights a week. Consequently, Toni-Ann and Neil's design priority was simple: Create a space that facilitates and celebrates sharing a meal with guests. This remodel was an opportunity to improve their life in a rich and fundamental way, and it was done without increasing the house's footprint. While the century-old Seattle house's existing kitchen was large enough, its poor layout, bad ventilation, minimal natural light, and cramped spaces made cooking a challenge.

In addition to improving the kitchen's utility, Toni-Ann and Neil wanted a healthy, green remodel that would pay homage to their 1900 home. Reusing existing flooring, lighting, and cabinet doors met those ends and also helped reduce construction costs. The new base cabinets use FSC-certified plywood with maple-veneer interiors and painted poplar frames. To minimize off-gassing, the plywood has no added urea formaldehyde. The new

trim matches that of the rest of the house to create a seamless transition between the old and the new. Improved ventilation, daylight, and a design that welcomes family and friends into the kitchen create an inspiring space Toni-Ann and Neil enjoy sharing.

Simple Changes Make a Big Impact

The greatest challenge with the original kitchen was the location of the stove in a peninsula that split the kitchen into a cooking area and a dinette. There was no ventilation above the stove, and neither side of the peninsula was roomy enough to serve effectively as a kitchen or a dining space. The kitchen was dark, and the upper cabinets crowded low over the counter, making food prep almost impossible. Cabinet space was minimal. The rear entry door swung in, devouring space, and the refrigerator was placed like an afterthought in a back corner.

Getting rid of the peninsula and moving the range to the south wall allowed for an exhaust hood and expanded the kitchen into what had been the

BEFORE

SPACE AND LIGHT.
Low upper cabinets,
few windows, and
a peninsula that
cut the room in half
made the old kitchen
feel small. Raising
the cabinets to the
ceiling, adding new
windows, and elimi-
nating the peninsula
made the remodeled
kitchen feel roomy
and bright.

BEFORE

OVERCOMING CHALLENGES. The stove was located in a peninsula that split the kitchen into a cooking area and a dinette, but neither side was roomy enough to serve their designated purposes. Getting rid of the peninsula and moving the range to the south wall expanded the kitchen into what had been the dinette.

dinette. Converting the mudroom entry to a pocket door made room for cabinets and a sink on the west wall, where daylight now floods the kitchen through an expansive sliding window. The window also provides a pass-through to the outside grill. Moving the bathroom door and reframing a couple of walls to recess the refrigerator into what had been an awkward hallway opened up the east end of the kitchen.

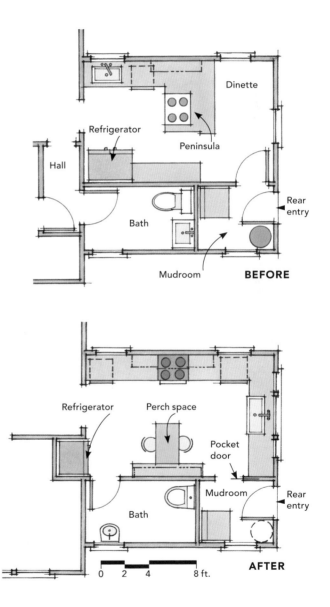

Dinette

Refrigerator

Peninsula

Hall

Rear entry

Bath

Mudroom

BEFORE

Refrigerator

Perch space

Pocket door

Mudroom

Rear entry

Bath

0 2 4 8 ft.

AFTER

STOLEN SPACE. Recessing the fridge into an adjacent hall and moving the bathroom door improved circulation and opened up new space. A new peninsula made from recycled studs created a "perch space" so that guests could be with the cook without being in the way. The chalkboard is a playful element that draws family and friends to that space.

Modern Made Comfortable

BY ERNIE RUSKEY

This house sits on a bluff with awe-inspiring views of Lake Champlain. My firm's goal was to create a modern home with Craftsman elements woven into the design of its exterior and interior. We wanted the home to have the comforts of traditional design but with the simplified and bright spaces associated with modern architecture.

The Craftsman influence can be seen on the exterior in the hip roofs, exposed timbers, and stonework. On the interior, the Craftsman influences are more modern: the use of materials in their natural state and the arrangement of them to create linear, understated spaces. This approach is clear in the kitchen.

SUCCESS ON ALL LEVELS. This contemporary kitchen benefits from a basic layout with wisely organized work zones and simple, refined materials presented in a clean composition.

CARVING OUT A KITCHEN
Defining spaces in a great room sometimes can be a challenge. Here are a few key strategies that were employed to make the kitchen and the surrounding spaces work together.

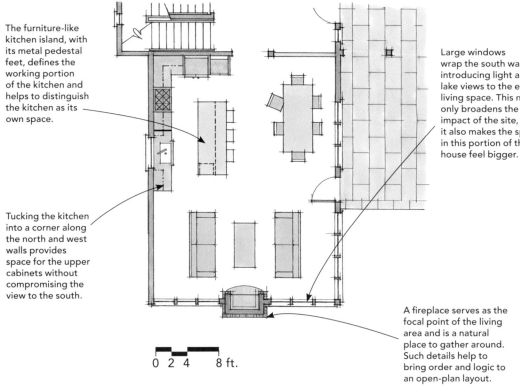

The furniture-like kitchen island, with its metal pedestal feet, defines the working portion of the kitchen and helps to distinguish the kitchen as its own space.

Tucking the kitchen into a corner along the north and west walls provides space for the upper cabinets without compromising the view to the south.

0 2 4   8 ft.

Large windows wrap the south wall, introducing light and lake views to the entire living space. This not only broadens the impact of the site, but it also makes the spaces in this portion of the house feel bigger.

A fireplace serves as the focal point of the living area and is a natural place to gather around. Such details help to bring order and logic to an open-plan layout.

The homeowners wanted a compact kitchen that would accommodate their passion for cooking, allow them to be part of the activity of the house, and provide them with access to the outdoor views that make the site so special to them.

A Place for Gathering

We designed the kitchen to be a workspace, which requires smooth circulation between the major zones: from areas for storage and prep, to spaces for cooking and cleaning up. Prep areas are organized as a tight triangle in the corner of the kitchen, while the cleanup zone is closer to the living room. This arrangement keeps the homeowners from being in each other's way when working together. Similarly,

the large maple-topped island is an intimate interaction point that doesn't encroach on the work areas. The island's overhang, which is supported by graceful metal brackets, and the stools set before it provide opportunities for casual dining and hanging out. The placement of the island in relation to the rest of the great room enables the homeowners to chat with family members and guests no matter whether they choose to gather at the island, in the dining room, or in the living room.

Subtle but Substantial Storage

The homeowners requested generous amounts of appropriately located storage. We set the refrigerator next to a large built-in double-door pantry in close

SHARED SPACE. The great room is composed of the living room, the dining room, and the kitchen, each of which blends into the others. A maple-topped island with a generous overhang defines the kitchen and provides a place for casual dining and entertaining.

proximity to the island, the kitchen's main prep surface. Open upper cabinets provide easy access to the dinnerware and to other kitchenware. These unpainted maple cabinets impart a refined yet casual feel to the kitchen. The island base, a combination of drawers, cabinets, and shelving for cookbooks, handles the bulk of the kitchen's day-to-day storage demands. The soffits hold items that get only occasional or seasonal use.

Timeless Design

The native-maple hardwood floors are durable, and they provide a visual link between all of the great-room spaces. The consistent floor plane throughout this area also helps to make the room feel larger than

it is. The same is true of the wall of windows that frames the views and casts the interior in daylight.

The color palette is a reflection of Vermont and of the home's immediate landscape. The cabinetry, trim, and tile backsplash fall into a soft blue-gray color scheme, analogous to the sky and to the lake in the distance.

A PALETTE APPROPRIATE TO HOUSE AND SITE. Light blue-gray cabinets complement the deep-blue glass tile backsplash, while black-granite countertops create contrast and durable worksurfaces. Stainless-steel appliances complete the kitchen's color scheme, which was driven by the colors of the view outside.

SOURCES

SINK
Franke®
Farm House
www.franke.com

FAUCET
Moen®
Level Series
www.moen.com

TILE
Island® Tile
Tile Breeze
www.islandtile.com

COUNTERTOP
Barre Tile
Honed Absolute Black Granite
www.barretile.com

CABINETS
DA Day Woodworks
Stowe, Vt.

CABINET PAINT
Benjamin Moore
Wedgwood Gray HC-146
www.benjaminmoore.com

PENDANT LIGHTS
West Elm
Globe Pendant
www.westelm.com

HARDWARE
Alno®
Contemporary
www.alnoinc.com

APPLIANCES
Jenn-Air Pro-Style
www.jennair.com

Going Toward the Light

BY ELIZABETH HERRMANN

Though untouched since it was built in the 1980s, this house had lots of potential. However, its lack of windows made the interior dark. It was a disjointed, compartmentalized building that paid surprisingly little attention to its surroundings. Knotty-pine paneling covered many of the house's small rooms. The new owners, who knew that the house was ripe for a redesign, hired me to create an open plan more suited to the lifestyle of a modern family.

Here, as in many homes, the kitchen is the hub, and it was crucial that it work just as well for large gatherings as for daily family routines. The key was to get rid of some interior walls, to add larger

BEFORE

REFLECT LIGHT, DON'T ABSORB IT. The new kitchen was the main beneficiary of a whole-house remodel that converted a dark and choppy interior into one that glows. White cabinets, bigger windows, light wood, and a contrasting dark-stained floor all contribute to the overall effect.

windows, and to brighten the interior—all while staying within a tight budget.

The homeowners also hired builder Red House of Burlington, Vt., to do the remodeling, which began with gutting the entire first floor. Together, we reconfigured the space to include a mudroom, large kitchen, living room, laundry, and half-bath.

Wood and Windows

The original house had a lot of wood in addition to the knotty-pine paneling, including some fir beams and a blond-oak floor. The flooring was still in good condition, but the finishes were worn, so we decided to refinish it with an ebony stain and water-based poly to unify the different areas of the floor plan. (We also stained the treads and risers with the same ebony color.) To brighten up the house, we replaced the pine wall paneling with drywall, or in the case of the stair wall, we chose to paint it white.

Around the kitchen, I specified new windows that match the style of the existing windows to help maintain an overall continuity to both the interior and the exterior. The new windows also made a huge difference in the amount of light reaching the interior. I located them to frame views of the

ISLAND-CENTRIC. A big, sturdy island with a thick Douglas-fir top is the family's favorite hangout spot before, during, and after meals. The mitered fir benches have nylon glides and easily slide out of the way when cooks need to stand at the island.

surrounding area that make the kitchen feel bigger. In particular, the massive 9-ft.-wide window in the kitchen looks out onto the Green Mountains and brings light deep into the house.

We used the kitchen's existing fir beam as a departure point and added one perpendicular to it to define the area around the island. To replace the bearing wall, Red House added a matching post and custom-made the beams' enameled-steel connecting hardware.

How the Kitchen Works

The kitchen design evolved out of discussions about family life and routines. This room needed to be a hardworking space flexible enough to accommodate diners at the island, an influx of guests, children doing homework, and two cooks at a time.

With an active family of five in the house, this kitchen had the potential for overcrowding if everyone gathered there at once. To keep the circulation open, we avoided dead ends, except in the organizational nook in the corner of the kitchen. The island, which functions as the heart of the house, has a 3-in.-thick Douglas-fir top that's finished with Watco® butcher-block oil. It serves as the breakfast table and homework desk, and when the benches are tucked underneath, it becomes a cook's workstation and chopping block.

Balancing the Cost

The most important budget guideline we used was to employ expensive materials just enough for the right function and impact. The pricey red Heath® ceramic tiles are a good example of what allowed me to add another layer of interest, link spaces, and create some fun highlights. We also had stainless-steel counter-tops fabricated to include a stainless-steel sink. They were expensive, but it's a great effect. Our many cost-saving measures included using metal cabinet drawers from Blum instead of custom wooden drawers, and refinishing the existing wood floor and stairs rather than replacing them.

ADDING OPEN SPACE

By removing interior walls in the old kitchen, the designer unified the kitchen and the living room, creating a more flexible space. A 130-sq.-ft. addition, used for dining, enlarged the overall space.

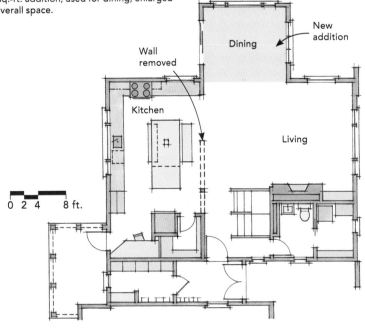

New addition

Dining

Wall removed

Kitchen

Living

0 2 4 8 ft.

PART OF A LARGER PLAN. Creating an open floor plan blended the living, dining, and kitchen areas into one relaxed space. The exposed fir beams convey a sense of scale. The open plan of the house creates access to lots of natural light.

SOURCES

LIGHT FIXTURES
(Island pendants)
West Elm
www.westelm.com

(Living-room pendant)
Criss Cross Bubble Lamp by
George Nelson
www.dwr.com

FLOOR FINISH
Ebony stain, finished with
DuraSeal® water-based poly
www.duraseal.com

WINDOWS
Andersen®
400 series
www.andersenwindows.com

COUNTERS
Metalworks
Custom stainless-steel around
the perimeter
www.metalworksvermont.com

SINK
Vigo®
www.vigoindustries.com

FAUCET
Grohe®
Concetto
www.grohe.com

RANGE
Blue Star®
36-in. Residential Nova Burner
gas range
www.bluestarcooking.com

REFRIGERATOR
Frigidaire
36-in.-wide Professional Series
refrigerator
www.frigidaire.com

SUBLIME SIMPLICITY. The remodel of this farmhouse kitchen in northwest Connecticut evokes lessons in traditional design to create a welcoming space that's bright and comfortable.

A Kitchen Built on Tradition

BY RAFE CHURCHILL

As the son of a second-generation master builder, I'm continuing a family legacy of creating traditional homes inspired by the historic architecture of New England and taking it further through work that responds to both the landscape and the specific needs of each client. My firm creates what has become known as the "new old house"—a building offering modern amenities, but with the scale, proportions, and textures of a historic home.

That approach to design and construction served as the foundation of this kitchen's redesign and reconstruction. The clients—a professional chef and an interior designer—wanted a new kitchen for their 1920s farmhouse that would have modern qualities as well as traditional ones to create a bright, welcoming, and comfortable atmosphere.

A CHEF'S KITCHEN
The client wanted the kitchen to function efficiently without spilling its prep areas into the dining area. In response, the range, refrigerator, and island are placed toward the north end of the kitchen, near the pantry. Meal prep and cooking can occur without too much interference, even when guests gravitate toward the island.

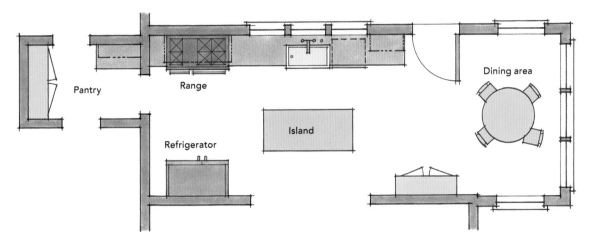

Pantry

Range

Refrigerator

Island

Dining area

BUILT FOR WORK. The kitchen's simplified arrangement doesn't come at the expense of functionality. A cook zone with a 48-in. Wolf range sits beneath a simply constructed custom hood. The schist backsplash extends to cover the entire wall surface behind the cooktop in order to make cleanup easy and to put its beautiful veining on display. Much of the kitchen's design is made possible by a pantry outfitted with floor-to-ceiling cabinetry. The pantry relieves the kitchen of an excess of upper cabinets and handles most of the bulk-food storage.

Understated Design

My favorite kitchens are those found in old abandoned houses or those found in vintage farmhouses that have been untouched by over-zealous remodelers. These kitchens were mostly built of freestanding cabinetry and simple wall-hung cupboards, and they included fully exposed appliances. Freestanding appliances imbue a kitchen with an unassuming simplicity, so we employ this design strategy where appropriate. In this kitchen, the range is built into the cabinetry, but a 48-in. stainless refrigerator with glass doors stands alone in the corner opposite the range. To make the kitchen appear older, we hung a single wall cupboard to the right of the sink to store glassware and introduced a shallow, freestanding hutch near the dining area for additional storage. In order to make so few upper cabinets possible, we relied on the nearby pantry cabinets, which are much larger, to handle the bulk of the kitchen's storage needs.

Sympathetic Surfaces

If there is one element within the kitchen that markedly establishes its country style, it's the paneling that covers the walls and ceiling, which were original to the farmhouse. Painted Benjamin Moore's Moonlight White, the paneling extends into the adjacent living areas of the home, creating a bright and continuous backdrop throughout the main floor. To complement the white walls, ceilings, and trim, we selected rift and quartersawn white-oak flooring and installed it throughout the pantry and the kitchen and into the living room. The flooring is light enough to keep the bright and open theme intact; plus it's durable, making it a good option for this dog-friendly home. We finished the flooring with Rubio® Monocoat, a unique hard-wax oil.

The countertops are the second-most prominent surface in the kitchen. The island top is made of 2-in.-thick premium wide-plank maple and has been oiled to give it a subtle contrast to the other

countertops in the kitchen, which are—to the surprise of many—not soapstone. They're actually schist and have a beautifully rich gray color with slight veining throughout.

Cabinetry and Color

The details of the few cabinets and the burst of color they impart on the space reflect some of our other kitchen designs, which these clients were drawn to. We turn to Shaker sensibilities when designing cabinets for our kitchens, and this can produce a more modern aesthetic. The cabinets are locally made and feature simple beaded face frames, flat-panel doors, and solid drawer fronts. Wooden knobs and chrome bin pulls keep the cabinetry balanced and unified with the paneling and flooring. The elements of this kitchen aren't competing for attention; rather, they are working together to create a simple space.

When it comes to color selections, I prefer colors that are more subdued and restrained. However, the clients presented tear sheets of various dream kitchens to use, and they kept gravitating toward one with light-blue cabinetry. In the end, they selected Farrow & Ball® Green Blue for all of the cabinetry in the kitchen. It's a more modern color selection, which adds to the way this kitchen presents traditional elements that feel firmly rooted in the present.

DESIGNED FOR LIVING. The kitchen's dining area is placed on the south end of the kitchen in front of a gable wall filled with glass. The area is drenched in daylight, which is reflected by the walls and ceiling of carefully restored planking painted a warm white and by newly installed white-oak flooring. Beyond its attentive layout, the kitchen balances beauty and comfort through carefully selected products and finishes.

SOURCES

CABINETS
Nichols Woodworking
Washington Depot, Conn.
www.shojiwood.com/
nichols

PENDANTS
(Dining)
CB2® Victory pendant
www.cb2.com

(Island)
Olde Good Things vintage
pendants
www.ogtstore.com

COUNTERTOPS
Schist
Rock Solid Marble &
Granite
Sheffield, Mass.
www.rocksolidmandg
.com

PAINT
(Cabinets)
Farrow & Ball Green Blue
www.farrow-ball.com

(Walls)
Benjamin Moore
Moonlight White
www.benjaminmoore
.com

Kesl Brothers Painting
Canton, Conn.
www.keslbrotherspainting
.com

SINK
Shaws Fireclay farm sink
www.rohlhome.com

RANGE
48-in. Wolf dual fuel
www.subzero-wolf.com

REFRIGERATOR
48-in. Sub-Zero
www.subzero-wolf.com

HARDWARE
(Bin pulls)
Restoration Hardware
www.restorationhardware
.com

(Wood knobs)
Shaker Workshops®
www.shakerworkshops
.com

FLOORING
5-in. rift and quartersawn
white oak
Franklin Wood Products

Rubio Monocoat clear
finish
www.rubiomonocoatusa
.com

Vintage Modern

BY NICOLE STARNES TAYLOR

Homeowners Jennifer Sargent and Matthew Cazier envisioned a light-filled kitchen with a clean-lined, modern aesthetic that still reflected the grace and charm of their 1918 house in the center of Seattle. Such a kitchen would welcome family and friends with sunlight and views to the garden. Its simple layout would be an inspiring backdrop for cooking and a welcome change to the existing kitchen's blend of outdated details.

Typical of kitchens a century ago, the existing room was dark, bare, separated from the rest of the house, and depressing. Although the cabinets were

SMALL CHANGES MAKE A BIG DIFFERENCE

The original location of the entries to the kitchen combined with the cabinet layout to create a traffic pinch point. The entry from the dining room was a narrow door that left the two rooms feeling separated. The original layout also placed the cook in the traffic flow. Moving and enlarging the dining-room entry and introducing a new cabinet layout solved these problems.

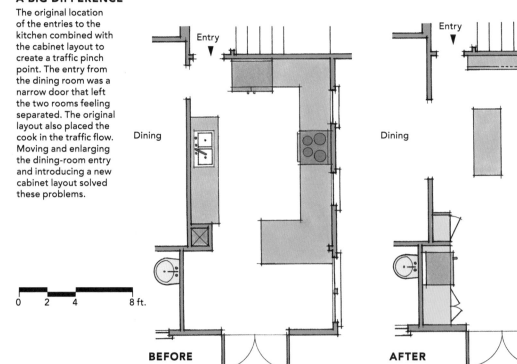

BEFORE

FIXING A GENERIC DESIGN AND AN AWKWARD FLOW. The low height of the main entry was changed to a more welcoming arch. Moving and enlarging the entry to the dining room opened up the plan and improved traffic flow, and new cabinets completely transformed the old kitchen.

MAKING NEW FIT OLD

BLENDING A CLEAN, MODERN AESTHETIC into an older house calls for details that reference the existing design as well as new features that harmonize rather than shock. One approach used here was to add some industrial details. Timeless and clean, the industrial look fits well with both the house's century-old roots and its owners' modern tastes.

1. Carrara-marble countertops offer a look that's clean but that also suggests the house's original era.
2. Black painted window frames and wall-mounted task lights look both industrial and chic, lending an informal air.
3. The extended-jamb detail eliminates casing and creates a more modern look.
4. The period-style faucet and sink reference the original house (photo, p. 199).
5. The coffered ceiling continues a detail from the dining room to help unite the spaces.
6. Shaker-style cabinets look traditional yet uncluttered.
7. A wall free of upper cabinets lends an open feel to the kitchen.
8. Deep pantry cabinets offer voluminous storage and allow for a sleek refrigerator installation.

fairly new, they were bland, and the layout divided the kitchen into a cooking area and a seating area that was rarely used. The entry was constricted, and the cabinet layout meant that the cook was always in the traffic flow. Despite these design issues, the house had been well cared for, and the rooms had wonderful scale and proportion. The spaces just needed some new life breathed into them.

Kitchens should allow people to celebrate the art of cooking and the joy of gathering and entertaining. I try to elevate the feel of a kitchen with details such as wood floors, coffered ceilings, and fancy lights. In an existing house, I look at the original details to see how to integrate the newly remodeled space with the original home. Next, I look for new details that can enliven the space and speak to the client's personality, aesthetic, and goals for the project. In kitchens, I find that adding an industrial bent keeps them from becoming precious and stuffy.

Open a Wall to Improve Flow and Feel

With general contractor Nicole Dumas doing the work, we replaced the small door between the kitchen and the dining room with a 6-ft.-wide cased opening to better connect the two rooms and to tie the kitchen visually to the rest of the house. At the other entry to the kitchen, we replaced the low, flat ceiling under the stair with an arch that followed the rise of the stair's stringers and added 8 in. to the ceiling height in the center. Not only is the arched opening in keeping with the historical period of the house, but it also makes the experience of entering the kitchen more dramatic.

By eliminating the peninsula and extending the kitchen into what had been the seating area, we increased storage without adding upper cabinets, helping to make this narrow room feel open and bright. An island made from an old wood table that Jennifer found at a neighborhood furniture store replaced the seating at the old peninsula. The table's

reclaimed wood brings texture and warmth to the kitchen. Nicole replaced the table's dilapidated wood top with Carrara marble, connecting it with the other countertops.

Blend Period Details with New

Carrying traditional details into the kitchen helped integrate the new space with the rest of the home. These include the faucet and the coffered ceiling, the baseboard, and the casing at the new opening between the dining room and the kitchen. The Shaker-style cabinets were painted on-site (Benjamin Moore Van Deusen Blue HC 156). While painting cabinets in the shop is often cheaper and can speed the job, painting on-site yields a superior end product. Every joint between shop-painted cabinets is painfully visible, and retouching dings from installation is extremely challenging. Particularly when working in old homes, painting on-site allows carpenters to employ all their tricks to make new cabinets fit seamlessly, even against an out-of-plumb wall. Prior to painting, joints between cabinets can be sanded flush, and small dings can be repaired.

The countertops and backsplashes are Carrara marble. A beautiful material with a traditional look, it is an excellent surface for rolling out dough, and at the end of a kitchen's life, it can be removed and reused. It requires annual sealing and prompt cleanup of spills, but even so, it will stain over time. Some view this as patina, while to others it's just staining. I provide samples for clients to slather up with such things as red wine, curry, mustard, and butter. This exercise has given many clients the confidence to install the material, and so far they all love it.

We broke with tradition along the exterior walls. To maximize views into the lush backyard, we replaced the old, standard height, French doors with 8-ft.-tall Marvin Integrity units. To bring in even more light, we placed headers high in the walls so the new windows could be installed with their tops as high as possible. The windows are painted black and depart from the traditional by having no casing. Instead, the jambs extend ¾ in. beyond the face of the wall. This 1× jamb is installed first, and then the drywall is mudded up to it. It's a tidy detail that we have done on several projects since.

Princeton Junior light fixtures from Schoolhouse Electric complete the industrial composition. These fixtures over the windows provide task lighting and offer an alternative to recessed lights. To keep the narrow kitchen feeling open and bright, we used no upper cabinets along the north wall. More sconces along this wall light work zones below and keep the wall from feeling overly long and unstructured. I like their jaunty, angular, never-perfect presence against that big white wall.

SOURCES

WINDOWS AND EXTERIOR DOORS
Marvin Windows and Doors
www.marvin.com

LIGHTS
Schoolhouse® Electric and Supply Co.
www.schoolhouseelectric.com

DISHWASHER
Bosch
www.bosch-home.com

FAUCET
Barber Wilsons and Co.
www.barwil.co.uk

STOVE
Blue Star
www.bluestarcooking.com

REFRIGERATOR
Liebherr
www.liebherr-appliances.com

SINK
Rohl
www.rohlhome.com

BRIGHT IDEA

With doors at opposite corners, the kitchen originally served as a pass-through between the main house and a breezeway leading to a separate garage wing. By adding a 100-sq.-ft. sunroom to the south side of the breezeway, Cate was able to move the doorway so that it lined up with the door from the living room. This shifts traffic to one side of the kitchen, making room for an uninterrupted U-shaped work area.

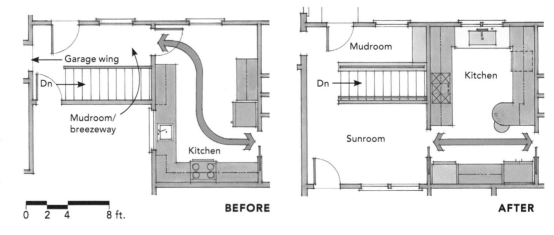

Garage wing

Dn

Mudroom/ breezeway

Kitchen

0   2   4   8 ft.

BEFORE

Mudroom

Dn

Kitchen

Sunroom

AFTER

A New Direction

BY CATE COMERFORD

The 1939 bungalow I'd purchased in Port Townsend, Wash., had a lot going for it, including great views of Admiralty Inlet and Puget Sound. Its kitchen, however, was another story. Situated between the living room and a mudroom linking the main house to a garage wing, the kitchen served as the pathway between those two structures and to the basement, the backyard, and the side yard. Getting to any of these places meant walking diagonally through the kitchen, which had come to feel like a hallway with some appliances arranged along it. I needed to change this traffic pattern, provide an uninterrupted space for two cooks, and arrange the appliances more efficiently.

Port Townsend is located in the rain shadow of the Olympic Mountains, so despite being in the Pacific Northwest, we get a surprising amount of sunny days. Adding a sunroom that faced south—overlooking the vegetable garden and offering a peekaboo view of Mount Rainier—not only made good design sense, but it also became the basis of a plan that would address my kitchen's traffic woes. I would line up the door into the new sunroom with

WALK THIS WAY. The doorway connecting the kitchen and the new sunroom repurposes the old swinging door from the mudroom as a sliding barn door.

the existing pocket door leading from the kitchen to the living room. Traffic between the house and the garage wing could now move straight across one end of the 10-ft.-wide kitchen without interfering with the work taking place there.

Out of Chaos, a Unified Workspace

Relocating the mudroom/breezeway door to the new sunroom allowed the creation of an efficient, U-shaped work area that local cabinetmaker Fred Kimball was able to outfit with cabinets following my design. The kitchen's original cabinets were plywood, built in place, and offered little to salvage beyond a wonderful old pullout cutting board that I had reinstalled in the new work area (photo, p. 209). There was one additional takeaway: The old cabinets had bright orange interiors, which made me smile every time I opened a door or drawer. When I got the new cabinets, I painted the interiors with the same cheerful color.

My new "U" space includes plenty of countertop work surfaces as well as the sink, dishwasher, and

FROM HALL TO MUDROOM. The mudroom's brick floor—repeated in the adjacent sunroom addition—contrasts nicely with the oak floor in the kitchen. A storage cabinet stands in the location of the kitchen's original entrance. A stair to the right leads to the basement.

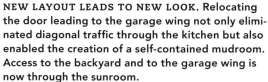

NEW LAYOUT LEADS TO NEW LOOK. Relocating the door leading to the garage wing not only eliminated diagonal traffic through the kitchen but also enabled the creation of a self-contained mudroom. Access to the backyard and to the garage wing is now through the sunroom.

gas cooktop. Upper cabinets hold dishes and pantry items; lower cabinets and drawers hold pots, pans, and cutting boards.

Traffic now flows past the far wall, where a built-in refrigerator/freezer and a combination oven, microwave, and warming drawer flank a hutch that contains a generous appliance garage. It may

not be a traditional work triangle, but I've found that this layout works great for my partner and me, who often cook at the same time. In particular, the refrigerator's position allows items to be taken out and staged on the nearby peninsula. When we're done cooking, those items are easily loaded back into the refrigerator.

Tough Countertops and Finishing Touches

The main countertops are made from bamboo flooring remnants by Bamboo Revolution of

PAINTED INTERIORS. Cate liked the cheerful vibe of the orange interiors of her old cabinets, so she painted the interiors of the new ones the same color—Benjamin Moore Buttered Yam AF-230.

Portland, Ore. The company fabricated the countertops as 1½-in.-thick slabs and shipped them to the site, where my contractor matched them to a template to fit the desired layout.

Port Townsend is the home of the School of Wooden Boat Building and the Wooden Boat

SLIDE-OUT CUTTING BOARD. A cutting board was the only piece of the old kitchen cabinets worth salvaging, and having it handy helps avoid inflicting damage on the bamboo countertops.

SMALL-APPLIANCE STORAGE. The toaster, mixer, coffeepot, and other small appliances are kept out of sight behind folding doors.

Festival, and many local carpenters work on boats as well as homes in town. For that reason, it's not surprising that my contractor suggested finishing the countertops with a marine spar varnish. This finish is not as brittle as other types of finishes and doesn't crack or chip. Although I've heard that almost all wood finishes are food-safe after fully curing, we continue to use cutting boards. The countertops clean up with soap and water followed by a dry cloth, and after three years, they still look great.

Countertops at the sink and in the appliance garage, where spills are more likely, are Carrara marble with a honed finish. At the sink, the 1¼-in.-thick marble is mounted on a plywood base and has a mitered lip that gives the illusion of a thicker slab.

RECLAIMED COUNTERTOP. Most of the countertops are reclaimed-bamboo slabs finished with marine varnish. But as an extra precaution against water damage, the sink is set in a 1¼-in.-thick slab of Carrara marble laid over plywood. A mitered lip in front gives the illusion of a thicker slab.

PETITE PENINSULA. A small, half-round peninsula offers a convenient place to perch as well as a staging area for food on its way in or out of the nearby refrigerator.

Although marble develops a patina over time, the stone I've used in my kitchen still looks almost new, despite three years of use.

Located over the sink is a restored vintage light fixture that I rescued years ago from the trash outside a historic home (photo p. 204). I had the fixture rewired and the metal parts dipped for a new, oil-rubbed bronze finish. For flooring, we decided to imitate the oak "shorts" used in the main part of the house. These leftover cuts, 8 in. to 12 in. long, are less expensive than traditional hardwood flooring. The new flooring was finished with Rubio Monocoat, a one-coat stain and finish system from Belgium that is water-resistant, has zero VOCs, and has held up remarkably well in our kitchen.

SOURCES

COUNTERTOPS
www.bamboorevolution.com

REFRIGERATOR
www.thermador.com

WALL-OVEN COMBO
www.thermador.com

CEILING LIGHTS
www.rejuvenation.com

FAUCET
www.rohlhome.com

SINK
www.kohler.com

FLOOR FINISH
www.rubiomonocoatusa.com

ANTIQUE-LIGHT RESTORATION
www.beckerindustries.com

Fit for
a Family

BY SCOTT TULAY

I n 2006, my wife and I purchased a 1,500-sq.-ft. cottage-style house in Amherst, Mass. Although the house was from the 1920s, its kitchen had been remodeled in the 1970s and was downright dysfunctional. We determined that the kitchen—along with every other room in the house—would have to be completely overhauled.

The original kitchen measured 11 ft. by 17 ft., with two short counters on opposing walls. With foot traffic running diagonally through the space, the kitchen was not conducive either to gathering or to cooking. There was no dedicated storage space, and the limited countertop area was taken up by a microwave, utensils, a toaster, a mixer, and a bread box. The cabinetry was old and broken down, there was no dishwasher, and—even though the daylight hardly penetrated it—it had only a single overhead light.

(*continued on p. 217*)

SAME FOOTPRINT, BETTER FUNCTION

With poor lighting, chaotic storage, and nowhere for lingering, the Tulays' kitchen was neither a comfortable gathering spot nor a satisfactory place in which to cook. Complicating the situation further was that traffic to the backyard cut diagonally through the space. This was solved by moving the back door. Adding windows and opening up the wall between the kitchen and the laundry room brought in more light. Clever custom storage was added to keep cooking supplies close at hand. With peninsula seating, there's now also a spot to do homework.

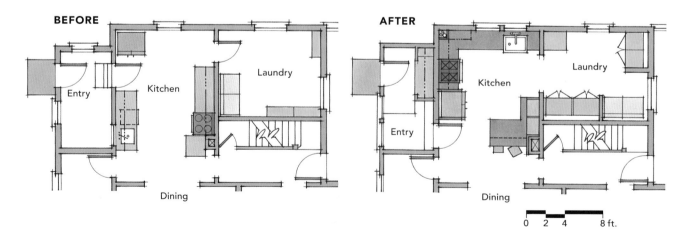

BEFORE · AFTER

Entry · Kitchen · Laundry · Dining

Entry · Kitchen · Laundry · Dining

0 2 4 8 ft.

A STORAGE WALL
THAT DOES IT ALL

BECAUSE HE WASN'T ADDING TO the footprint of the kitchen, Scott knew that whatever storage space he carved out would have to be extremely functional. The kitchen's interior wall offered lots of potential but also presented two challenges. The first was that locating the peninsula there would make it difficult to reach the storage above. Cabinetmaker Jim Picardi suggested outfitting the cabinets with shelving units from Rev-A-Shelf that pull down to bring items within reach. To be sure that these shelving units would be accessible, Scott made a full-size cardboard mock-up of the peninsula and measured his wife's reach to make sure she could grab the handles.

The second challenge was a furnace chimney inside the wall that left only about 3 in. of useful space in front of it. To put this thin space to good use, Scott designed a shallow cabinet with pockets for school papers and a charging station for mobile devices (photo, p. 216). A long power strip on the back side of the peninsula allows laptops to be plugged in when someone is working there. Other features of the wall include appliance garages, trash and recycling bins under the peninsula, and a deep drawer under the microwave to keep saucepans and lids organized (photo, p. 217).

KITCHEN CENTRAL. Cabinets designed by the author and cabinetmaker Jim Picardi incorporate storage and a peninsula. A shallow cabinet built over a brick chimney is just the right depth for school papers and electronic devices (facing page), and a deep drawer under the microwave, outfitted with dividers from Rev-A-Shelf, keeps saucepans and lids organized (above).

We had several goals for our kitchen remodel: to improve the traffic pattern, to increase daylight, and to make the space feel more welcoming. Given our budget, we chose not to enlarge the kitchen. We did, however, decide to expand the opening to an adjacent pantry and laundry room that, because of its narrow door, felt hidden away.

Focused on the Family

To be sure I got the functionality right in the remodel, I asked my wife and daughters about how they used the kitchen, and then I observed them doing just that. I noticed that when my wife was cooking, she would have to walk over to the opposite counter whenever she needed a utensil. Spices and pot holders also required trips back and forth. With no garbage disposal and the trash can located in the back pantry, there were frequent trips to discard food waste and packaging. It became clear that the redesign should bring these areas within closer reach.

I also noticed that while my wife and I prepared dinner, our daughters often would trek downstairs from their rooms to ask for homework help. I decided to design a peninsula where they could do their homework. Along with moving the entry door, this peninsula would create a separation between the new kitchen work area and traffic coming through the back door to the rest of the house. At the same time, however, it would require a creative approach to ensuring access to the cabinets above it (see "A Storage Wall That Does It All," p. 214).

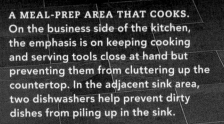

A MEAL-PREP AREA THAT COOKS.
On the business side of the kitchen,
the emphasis is on keeping cooking
and serving tools close at hand but
preventing them from cluttering up the
countertop. In the adjacent sink area,
two dishwashers help prevent dirty
dishes from piling up in the sink.

Lightening It Up

To remedy the lack of natural light, I added a window to the adjacent south-facing entry hall. I also decided to add more glass by asking local cabinetmaker Jim Picardi to build a custom door to the kitchen from the entry so that southern light could enter the kitchen for most of the day.

Enlarging the entrance to the laundry room and pantry also brought in more light and made the kitchen itself feel bigger. To help the two spaces feel like one, we matched the crown molding, window trim, and hardware in the laundry/pantry with that in the kitchen, even though we used off-the-shelf cabinets in the laundry/pantry to save money. Finally, we added two single windows near the sink's new location, allowing in more sunlight and a view outdoors from the sink.

Custom Solutions Make It All Work

Given the kitchen's small footprint and our desire to maximize storage, it was clear that custom cabinets would be a wise investment. Jim and I worked hard to add functionality to every cabinet and to utilize every square inch of space. Another goal was to minimize clutter by clearing the countertops of appliances when not in use, so I integrated appliance garages into the cabinetry on top of the counter. These allow us to slide the coffeemaker, the mixer, and the toaster out when needed and then hide them away when not in use.

CUSTOMIZED FOR COOKING. Drawers containing cooking and serving supplies surround the 30-in. KitchenAid dual-fuel range. A shallow drawer to the right organizes silverware and other utensils using spring-loaded stainless-steel dividers from Blum. Below it, a deeper drawer outfitted with a customizable pegboard keeps bowls and plates in order. To the left of the range, a custom drawer fitted with restaurant-style utensil canisters puts cooking tools where they're needed while keeping them out of sight when they're not.

Finally, I decided to place a small dishwasher on one side of the sink for small loads, and a full-size dishwasher on the other side for larger loads. Having two dishwashers allows the sink to be relatively clear of dirty dishes at all times and helps keep the kitchen looking open and clean.

SOURCES

STOOLS
Recycled wood seats on
industrial stool bases
www.sticksandbricksshop.com

PENDANTS
Eleek Starlight in recycled
aluminum
www.eleekinc.com

BACKSPLASH
Recycled aluminum 2×6 tiles in
three finishes
www.naturalbuilthome.com

FLOOR
12×12 natural-cleft
Brazilian-slate tiles
www.arrowtiles.com

FAUCET
Jaclo® dual-articulated
satin-nickel bridge
www.Jaclo.com

SINK
Shaws Original fireclay apron
farmhouse sink
www.rohlhome.com

COUNTERTOPS
Jet mist granite, honed finish
www.vermontstructuralslate.com

To the Studs and Back

BY LAUREN AND KYLE ZERBEY

Our house was built in 1910, and although it was Craftsman in style, its small size and lack of custom details led us to believe that it was originally a worker's cottage. Because of its modest square footage, the kitchen was effectively the hallway of the home—with five doorways adding chaos to its inefficiency.

We lived in our home for four years before tackling the kitchen, which gave us ample time to design and redesign it until we got everything just the way we wanted. By taking the space down to the studs, we were able to move the kitchen toward the back of the house and take over an enclosed porch that was rarely used. Not only did this free up space

CEILING THE DEAL. Transitions between open-plan areas were handled by varying the ceiling form. By vaulting the ceiling over the kitchen and dining area and adding new windows and a pair of skylights, the Zerbeys ensured that there would be enough natural light—even on cloudy days—that they rarely would need to turn on the lights.

BACK ON TRACK

Before the remodel, the kitchen was effectively the hallway, and its five doorways bottlenecked the space. The Zerbeys' vision was to open up the living spaces to each other. By surrendering a rarely used enclosed porch, they were able to move the kitchen to the back of the house and create a better visual and physical connection to the backyard.

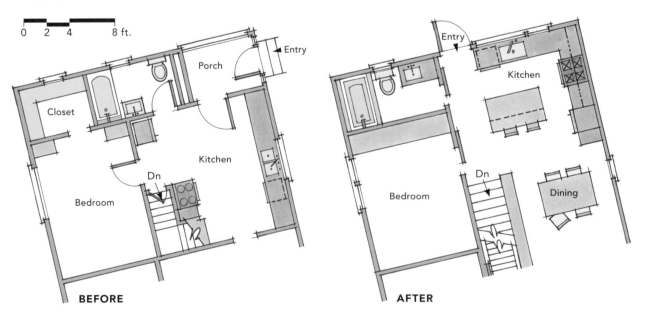

in the rest of the house by allowing us to shuffle rooms around and squeeze in a second bedroom, but it also created a better visual and physical connection to the backyard.

The kitchen had been "remuddled" in the 1960s. The range was placed where the original woodstove had been, and next to that was a fake cabinet that provided head clearance for a stair down to the basement. A freestanding fridge was located in another corner, and the sink was barely large enough to wash pots and pans in. Soon after moving in, we sacrificed the one bank of drawers the kitchen had to put in a dishwasher, but that was only the beginning of greater changes to come.

As architects, we chose to do most of the work ourselves. Not only was that a way to afford the remodel, but it was also an opportunity to have more hands-on experience with residential construction. Fortunately, Kyle had inherited his grandfather's tool collection, which gave us a huge boost.

The main objective for remodeling our home was to maximize its space and to create functional and inviting areas with plenty of natural light. One way we handled transitions between these areas was to vary the ceiling form. Over the living area, we exposed the original joists; over the kitchen and dining area, we vaulted the ceiling. New windows and a pair of skylights ensure that we rarely need to turn the lights on, even on the cloudiest of Seattle days.

The kitchen is the workhorse of our house, and the materials and products we chose reflect that. We call our aesthetic *natural modernism*—warm woods, bright whites, cool grays—a style that's minimal without being overly austere or impractical. We were able to stay within budget and distinguish our space by modifying a number of readily available items.

Although we used Ikea cabinets, we incorporated our own open shelving for a more customized look. Fir plywood wraps the side and top of one wall of cabinets to create a stronger composition and to better define that zone. The island is a pair of Ikea drawer units with a custom shelf. The cavity under

BUDGET CUSTOM. Ikea cabinets were integrated with open shelving the Zerbeys built to create a more customized look. Fir plywood on the side and top of one wall of cabinets helps to define that zone.

CLEVER ISLAND ASSEMBLY. The butcher-block island top was made by butting together two counter-depth pieces. The base is made from a pair of Ikea drawer units. Custom shelves at one end hold the microwave and bowls for the dog's food and water.

WARM AND SIMPLE. The Zerbeys describe their design aesthetic as natural modernism, a style that's clean, practical, and simple, but not too stark.

the island serves as a plenum for heating using a toe-kick register.

We wanted to use butcher block on the island but found that a slab in the size we needed would have been cost-prohibitive. Instead, we butted two standard counter-depth pieces together to create one larger piece on which the seam is barely visible.

Behind the range, we created a simple backsplash with back-painted glass and aluminum channel trim on the exposed sides. A metal picture ledge above it works as shallow storage for everyday items. Under the sink, four pullout bins serve as receptacles for trash, recycling, compost, and dog food.

Opening up the spaces dramatically transformed the feel and flow of the home. By sticking to a neutral theme, with a focus on the architecture itself, we used art, accessories, and paint to add color and texture—a move that allows us to change the mood of the space easily.

Our strategy with our own home, as with the homes of many of our clients, was to strike a balance between design and value. In hindsight, we would have done few things differently.

SOURCES

CABINETS
Ikea
Akurum with Abstrakt
fronts
www.ikea.com

DRAWER AND DOOR PULLS
Reveal Designs®
www.reveal-designs.com

FLOORING
Capri Cork®
Mediterra Dark
www.capricork.com

COUNTERS
Silestone
White North
www.silestoneusa.com

ISLAND COUNTER
Cross Cut Hardwoods
Lyptus
www.crosscuthardwoods
.com

SINK
Kräus
stainless-steel single basin
www.kraususa.com

FAUCET
Grohe
Minta in SuperSteel
www.grohe.com

LIGHT FIXTURES
(Wall)
Resolute®
Purity Reach
www.resoluteonline.com

(Island)
Bruck®
VIA Linear Chandelier
www.brucklighting.com

(Undercabinet)
ET2®
LED tape lights
www.et2online.com

RANGE
GE
Cafe 30-in. dual fuel
www.geappliances.com

DISHWASHER
Bosch
SHX46L
www.bosch-home.com

REFRIGERATOR
Liebherr
30-in. Liebherr
www.liebherr-appliances
.com

MICROWAVE
GE
Spacemaker II
www.geappliances.com

RANGE HOOD
Vent-A-Hood
PRH9-230
www.ventahood.com

BARSTOOLS
Ikea
Sebastian
www.ikea.com

METAL LEDGE
West Elm
www.westelm.com

A Perfect Kitchen Grows Up

BY SOPHIE PIESSE

Had someone asked me about my kitchen in 1999, I would have said it was perfect. As a centerpiece of the new home we had just built, it met the particular needs of myself and my husband. Even several years later when our first son was born, the space continued to fit us perfectly. In fact, it matched our lifestyle so well that it was written up in two magazines as a prime example of a comfortable, functional, family-friendly kitchen.

This kitchen that we had designed for ourselves as first-time homeowners on a very tight budget had served us well when we needed little more than a modest but comfortable kitchen, centrally located, near the entry to the house. At the time, we also wanted a home with an open plan that incorporated the living and dining areas, brought in ample daylight, and felt connected to the outdoors. We wanted it to be affordable and as green as possible.

To control some of the costs, we assembled and installed the Ikea cabinets ourselves, and we chose laminate counters. We got some great deals on appliances, which allowed us to splurge on a tall and very energy-efficient 14-cu.-ft. ConServ® refrigerator/freezer. In 1999, it was way ahead of the

2014

PRIORITIES CHANGE, A KITCHEN ADAPTS. The author's original kitchen, featured in *Inspired House* magazine in 2004, was a cozy space carefully planned to complement the lifestyle of a family just starting out. Years later, with two growing sons in the family, the kitchen needed to grow up, too. Keeping within the same footprint, the author enlarged the island to accommodate multiple cooks and activities while adding a coffee bar, a larger refrigerator, more storage, and a deeper sink. A more contemporary, sophisticated palette emphasizes the new family dynamic.

2004

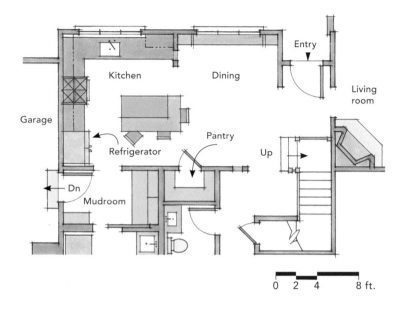

curve on efficiency, and its compact size worked well for a couple, and even a family of three.

Kitchens Need to Grow, Too

Fast-forward to 2014. That first son had become an active 13-year-old, with a younger brother who was all energy. We'd already remodeled much of the house (adding a playroom and an expanded mudroom) to match the new family dynamic, but we also reached the conclusion that our kitchen wasn't quite as perfect as it once had been.

As a residential architect, I renovate a lot of kitchens. The conversations I have with my clients always focus on how the kitchen serves the family and how it should complement their lives. But what I also discuss with them—and what I now needed to talk about with my own family—is how our kitchens need to grow with us.

Good Bones, but Different Needs

Fifteen years later, the kitchen's basic layout still worked great, as did the lighting, the appliance locations, the size, and the connection to the rest of the house and to the outdoors. But the kitchen now served a busy family of four. Our two boys enjoy

CROWD PLEASER. The new "coffee altar" keeps hot-beverage supplies neat but accessible behind a stainless tambour door. Mugs, cups, and saucers reside in the drawer below.

CABINET COLLABORATION. Designed by the author to maximize function, the cabinets were built by Mark Burford and mix glass doors from Ikea's Jutis line with doors and drawer fronts made from stranded bamboo (www.plyboo.com). The floor is the original colored concrete, accented by a new rug that was designed by the author using carpet tiles from Flor (www.flor.com). The backsplash tiles are from the Crystile Wave series.

AN ISLAND EXPANDS

THE ORIGINAL KITCHEN ISLAND MEASURED 36 in. by 48 in. and included seating for two. It had a 15-in. drawer stack and a sink cabinet. (The island was plumbed for a prep sink that proved to be unnecessary.) Redesigned, it now measures 39 in. by 68 in. and has comfortable seating for four. The waterfall countertop is striking and shows off the beauty of both the Environite and the stranded bamboo as it flows from one end to the other. (It also helps to stop legs from sticking out into the traffic flow.) The island incorporates an easily accessible duplex outlet; a pullout chopping board; and drawer storage for knives, mixing bowls, measuring spoons, Tupperware®, towels, and utensils. A separate drawer is dedicated to plastic wrap, tin foil, and other school-lunch needs. The new orientation makes meal prep very efficient, with the sink, dish drawers, and a large drawer for small appliances all located within a few steps of a lovely large island top to spread everything out on.

helping us cook, and we all love to entertain and to hang out in the kitchen.

We now needed workstations for multiple cooks and a serious increase in our food-storage capacity. Young boys, it seems, eat their weight in food every week, and teenage boys eat twice that. It soon became clear that we needed a much larger fridge, and a bigger cooktop and sink.

We found the original kitchen lacking in a few other areas: Standardized Ikea cabinetry did not provide the most efficient use of space, especially in our small kitchen. We needed more functional, easily accessible storage. Cheaper materials (cabinets and countertops, lighting, appliances) fit our budget at the time, but now that we were planning to stay in this house for the long haul, many of those items needed to be replaced.

Similar Goals, New Priorities

We still wanted to select environmentally friendly materials and energy-efficient appliances, and we also still felt the need to be fiscally responsible.

Keeping the same space but using it better enabled us to do both. We didn't move any doors or windows, and we kept the original floor, a colored-concrete radiant slab on grade. This allowed us to focus our creativity and resources elsewhere. We splurged on locally made recycled-glass countertops (www.environite.com), stranded bamboo cabinets, and aluminum-laminate toe kicks (www.richelieu.com), which make the cabinets seem to float.

Retaining the layout also allowed us to focus on making our cabinets function better. We designed a storage area over the fridge to accommodate our baking trays, tins, and platters, and another to store frying pans vertically alongside the range. We installed a two-tier spice drawer as well as an organized space for utensils, knives, trivets, and gadgets. Dishes moved to a base-cabinet drawer so that the kids can easily unpack the adjacent

dishwasher. An extralarge (33-in. by 18-in. by 10-in.) sink (www.ukinox.com) keeps soaking dishes hidden.

I dislike lazy Susans, so I used the corner cabinet for a trash pullout. It fits two 35-qt. bins for trash and recycling, with room on the side for dish towels. The cabinet pulls out diagonally on full-extension slides and is equipped with a toe hole in the bottom for hands-free operation.

Our favorite addition is our "coffee altar," a garage with everything needed for coffee or tea. Mugs, cups, and saucers are stored directly below.

Finally, we reoriented and expanded the island (which originally sat only two people) to seat our whole family comfortably. It has since become our primary workstation (see "An Island Expands," on the facing page).

Do these changes mean that our kitchen was not so perfect the first time? Not necessarily. It was a great kitchen for who we were then. But I have grown as a mother and an architect, and my kitchen needed to do the same. Like our family, the kitchen has matured to reflect our style and our needs today—and hopefully for many more years to come.

CONTRIBUTORS

Don Burgard is senior copy/production editor at *Fine Homebuilding*.

Anatole Burkin is a freelance writer in Santa Rosa, Calif.

Rafe Churchill is a designer in Sharon, Conn.

Cate Comerford's architectural practice focuses on historic restoration, renovation, and traditional design.

Jim Compton is an architect in Raleigh, N.C.

Bud Dietrich, AIA, is an architect and writer (hfdarchitects.com) in New Port Richey, Fla.

Jeffrey R. Dross is a corporate director for education and industry trends at Kichler Lighting.

Andy Engel is a senior editor at *Fine Homebuilding*.

David Getts (davidgettsdesign.com) is a carpenter and freelance writer in Seattle.

Jamie Gold, CKD, CAPS, is a kitchen designer in San Diego and the author of *New Kitchen Ideas that Work* (Taunton Press, 2012) and the upcoming *New Bathroom Idea Book* (Taunton Press, 2017).

Sean Groom is a contributing editor to *Fine Homebuilding*.

Philip Hansell (hansellpainting.com) is a painter in Durham, N.C.

Elizabeth Herrmann practices architecture in Bristol, Vt.

Matt Higgins is social media editor at *Fine Homebuilding*.

Reid Highley (candharch.com) is an architect in Hillsborough, N.C.

Tim Keefe is a tile installer in Dedham, Mass.

Brent Kelosky is vice president of Wood Floor Designs in Koppel, Pa.

Joseph B. Lanza lives in Duxbury, Mass. His website is josephlanza.com.

Nena Donovan Levine is a kitchen designer in West Hartford, Conn.

Isaak Mester has been in the construction business for 30 years. Although he has tackled all phases of residential construction, he has concentrated on kitchens and baths during the last 10 years. In an acknowledgment of his sore shoulders and knees, Isaak has become a licensed building and plumbing inspector.

Sophie Piesse is the principal and owner of Sophie Piesse, Architect P.A. (sophiepiesse.com), a company she founded in 2006. Her practice specializes in residential, sustainable design and a unique collaborative approach that empowers her builders and clients to create beautiful, functional, and thoughtful spaces. She has been designing valuable real-world solutions in the residential home industry for over 20 years. Sophie, an Australian transplant, currently resides in Carrboro, N.C.

Ernie Ruskey is the owner and principal of Tektonika Studio Architects in Stowe, Vt.

Debra Judge Silber is the former managing editor at *Fine Homebuilding*.

Architect and former carpenter **Nicole Starnes Taylor** owns MAKE Design Studio (makedesignstudiollc.com) in Seattle.

Gary Striegler is a master trim carpenter from Fayetteville, Ark.

Scott Tulay is an architect in Amherst, Mass.

David O'Brien Wagner is an architect at SALA Architects in Minneapolis.

Originally from Olympia, Wash., **Kevin Ward** grew up in a flooring family; after college, he took on construction and, subsequently, flooring jobs, which led to a partnership with a friend in a hardwood flooring business. In 2010, Kevin moved to Austin, Texas, where he is the installation supervisor with custom-flooring manufacturer Hardwood Designs.

Lauren and Kyle Zerbey run Studio Zerbey, an architecture and design firm in Seattle.

CREDITS

All photos are courtesy of *Fine Homebuilding* magazine © The Taunton Press, Inc., except as noted below.

The articles in this book appeared in the following issues of *Fine Homebuilding*:

pp. 5–8: Drawing Board: Opening Up a Kitchen by Reid Highley and Jim Compton, issue 247. Drawings by Jim Compton.

pp. 9–11: Drawing Board: Zones for Small Appliances by Bud Dietrich, issue 239. Drawings by Bud Dietrich.

pp. 12–19: A Designer's Guide to Countertops by Jamie Gold, issue 239. Photos by Rodney Diaz, except for photo p. 13 courtesy of Jamie Gold and photos p. 16 and 17 by Greg Riegler.

pp. 20–25: Countertop Chemistry by Debra Judge Silber, issue 255. Photos by John Gruen, except for photo p. 22 by Adrienne Breaux and photo pp. 24–25 Rodney Diaz.

pp. 26–30: A Bolder Backsplash by Anatole Burkin, issue 255. Photos courtesy of Bendheim, except for photo p. 27 by Brian Vanden Brink.

pp. 31–38: Kitchens Illuminated by Jeffrey R. Dross, issue 239. Photos by Charles Bickford, except for photos p. 34 by Charles Miller. Drawings by Christopher Mills.

pp. 40–46: Undercabinet Lighting Is Better than Ever by Debra Judge Silber, issue 241. Photos by Rodney Diaz, except for photo p. 40 by Rob Yagid, photo p. 43 courtesy of Eric Gjerde, and photo botom left p. 45 courtesy of Tech Lighting.

pp. 47–53: Ready-to-Assemble Kitchen Cabinets by Anatole Burkin, issue 255. Photos by Debra Judge Silber, except for photo p. 47 courtesy of Ikea.

pp. 54–64: Get to Know Semi-custom Cabinets by Nena Donovan Levine, issue 242. Photos p. 58 courtesy of Aristokraft, photos p. 55, 56 top, and 61 courtesy of Canyon Creek, photo p. 57 right courtesy of Diamond, photos p. 57 left, 62, and 63 courtesy of Master-Brand, photos p. 56 bottom, 59, and 60 courtesy of Merillat, photo p. 58 bottom courtesy of Omega.

pp. 65–73: Best-Value Appliances by Sean Groom, issue 247. Photos courtesy of the manufacturers.

pp. 74–75: What's the Difference: Electric Ovens by Don Burgard, issue 239. Drawings by Trevor Johnston.

pp. 76–78: What's the Difference: Drinking Water Filtration Systems by Don Burgard, issue 253. Photo p. 76 courtesy of Bed Bath & Beyond, photo p. 77 left courtesy of Pur, photo p. 77 right courtesy of Aquasana, and photo p. 78 courtesy of Environmental Water Systems.

pp. 79–86: A Closer Look at Solid-Wood Flooring by Anatole Burkin, issue 257. Photos by Rodney Diaz, except for photos pp. 80–81, 83 bottom right by Susan Teare, photo p. 82 bottom left by Aaron Fagan, photo p. 83 bottom left by Charles Bickford, and photo p. 85 by Justin Fink.

pp. 87–89: What's the Difference: Linoleum vs. Vinyl by Matt Higgins, issue 256. Product photos by Dan Thornton; installation photos courtesy of Armstrong.

pp. 91–97: Refinish Your Cabinets by Phillip Hansel, issue 240. Photos by Patrick McCombe.

pp. 98–107: Installing Semicustom Cabinets by Isaak Mester, issue 241. Photos by Charles Bickford, except for photo p. 101 top by John Ross. Drawing by Dan Thornton.

pp. 108–111: A Clever Island with Drawers by Joseph B. Lanza, issue 239. Photos by Charles Bickford. Drawings by John Hartman.

pp. 112–119: Crown Molding for Kitchen Cabinets by Gary Striegler, issue 244. Photos by Andy Engel, except for p. 113 by Bryan Striegler. Drawings by Bob La Pointe.

pp. 120–128: A Pro Approach to Tiling a Backsplash by Tim Keefe, issue 247. Photos by Justin Fink, except for photo p. 121 by Michael Piazza. Drawings by John Hartman.

pp. 129–131: Building Skills: Cut a Laminate Counterop for a Sink by Andy Engel, issue 242. Process photos by Patrick McCombe; product photos by Dan Thornton.

pp. 132–138: Refinish Your Wood Floors by Brent Kelosky, issue 253. Photos by Justin Fink.

pp. 139–145: Wood Floors on a Concrete Slab by Kevin Ward, issue 246. Photos by Charles Bickford, except for photo p. 140 top left courtesy of Lignomat and photo p. 140 top right courtesy of Tramex.

pp. 147–154: Universal Appeal by Debra Judge Silber, issue 239. Photos by Craig Thompson, except for photo p. 150 top and 152 top left courtesy of Crown Point Cabinetry/ Jeffrey Stowell. Drawings by Martha Garstang Hill.

pp. 155–162: Surgical Kitchen Remodel by David Getts, issue 236. Photos by Charles Bickford, except for photo p. 156 by Benjamin Benschneider.

pp. 163–168: Kitchen, Meet Dining Room by Nicole Starnes Taylor, issue 240. Before photos courtesy of Nicole Starnes Taylor; all other photos by Aaron Leitz. Drawings by Martha Garstang Hill.

pp. 169–174: Tasteful Transformation by David O'Brien Wagner, issue 247. Photos by Troy Thies, except for photo p. 169 courtesy of David O'Brien Wagner. Drawings by Martha Garstang Hill.

pp. 175–180: Same Space, Twice the Room by Nicole by Starnes Taylor, issue 247. Before photos by Nicole Dumas; all other photos by Aaron Leitz. Drawings by Martha Garstang Hill.

pp. 181–185: Modern Made Comfortable by Ernie Ruskey, issue 247. Photos by Susan Teare. Drawing by Martha Garstang Hill.

pp. 186–191: Going Toward the Light by Elizabeth Herrmann, issue 247. Photos by Susan Teare, except for photo p. 187 top courtesy of Elizabeth Herrmann. Drawing by Martha Garstang Hill.

pp. 192–197: A Kitchen Built on Tradition by Rafe Churchill, issue 250. Photos by John Gruen. Drawing by Martha Garstang Hill.

pp. 198–203: Vintage Modern by Nicole Starnes Taylor, issue 255. Photos by Aaron Leitz, except for photo p. 199 bottom courtesy of Nicole Starnes Taylor. Drawings by Martha Garstang Hill.

pp. 204–211: A New Direction by Cate Comerford, issue 255. Photos by Matthew Varnado. Drawings by Martha Garstang Hill.

pp. 212–220: Fit for a Family by Scott Tulay, issue 255. Photos by Nat Rea. Drawings by Martha Garstang Hill.

pp. 221–225: To the Studs and Back by Lauren and Kyle Zerbey, issue 255. Photos by Lauren Zerbey. Drawings by Martha Garstang Hill.

pp. 226–231: A Perfect Kitchen Grows Up by Sophie Piesse, issue 255. Photos by Sophie Piesse, except for photo p. 227 right by Steve Cash. Drawings by Martha Garstang Hill.

INDEX